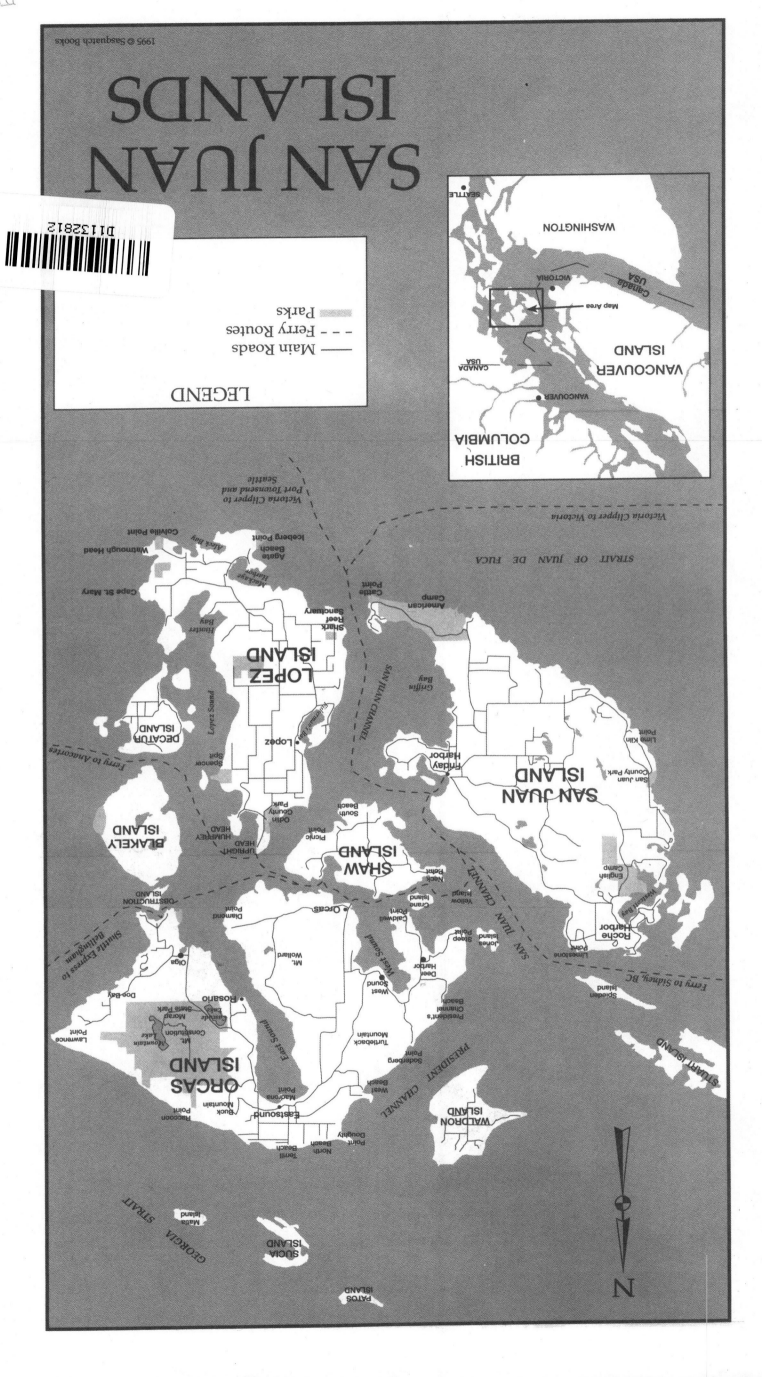

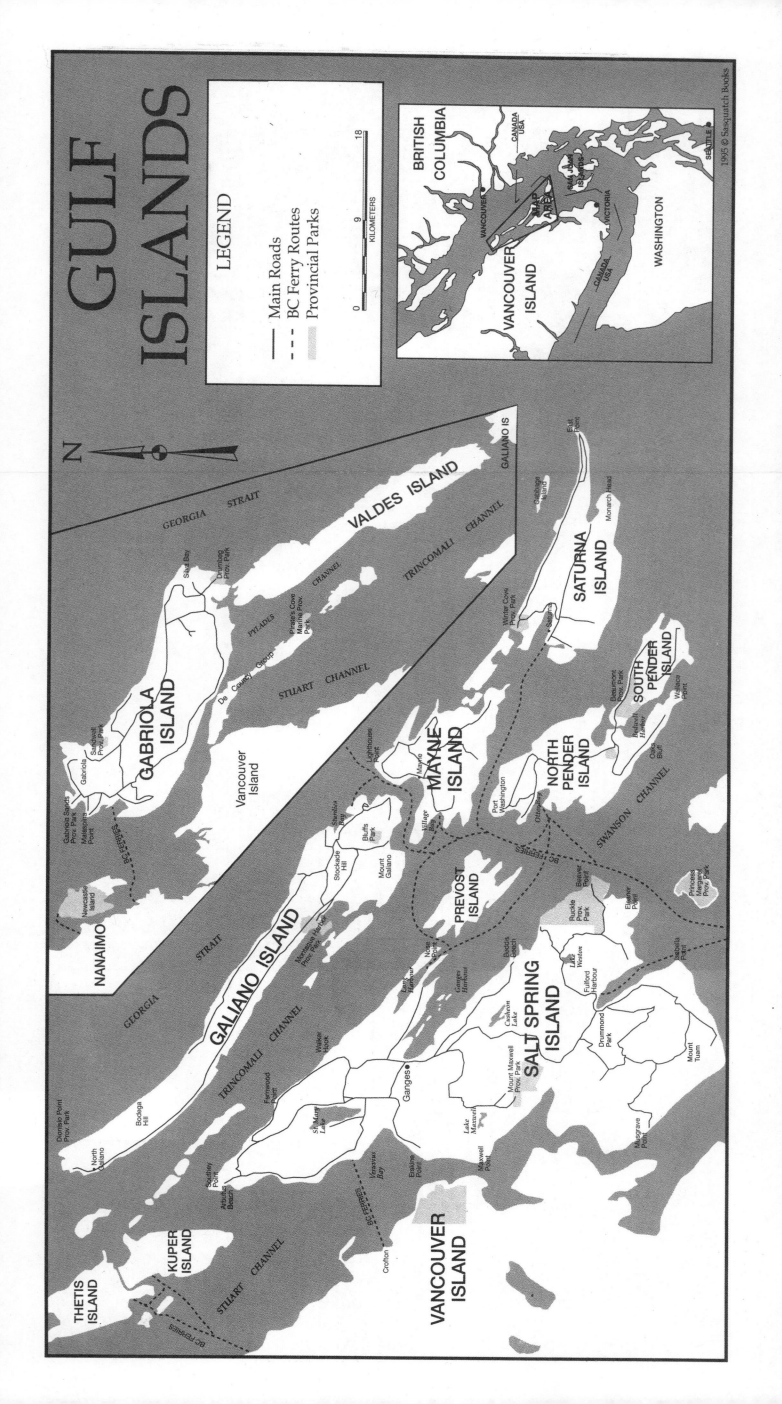

SAN JUAN &
GULF ISLANDS

BEST PLACES®
DESTINATIONS

SAN JUAN & GULF ISLANDS

2ND EDITION

EDITED BY JAN HALLIDAY

SASQUATCH BOOKS
SEATTLE

Printed in the United States of America.
Published in the United States by Sasquatch Books
Distributed in Canada by Raincoast Books
Second edition
06 05 04 03 02 01 00   5 4 3 2 1

Series editor: Kate Rogers
Assistant editor: Justine Matthies
Cover design: Nancy Gellos
Cover photo: ©Joel W. Rogers/CORBIS
Foldout map: Word Graphics
Interior design adaptation and composition: Fay Bartels,
Kate Basart, Millie Beard, and Dan McComb

ISSN: 1525-6553
ISBN: 1-57061-231-5

SASQUATCH BOOKS
615 Second Avenue
Seattle, WA 98104
(206)467-4300
books@SasquatchBooks.com
http://www.SasquatchBooks.com

Special Sales

BEST PLACES® guidebooks are available at special discounts on bulk purchases for corporate, club, or organization sales promotions, premiums, and gifts. Special editions, including personalized covers, excerpts of existing guides, and corporate imprints, can be created in large quantities for specific needs. For more information, contact your local bookseller or Special Sales, Best Places Guidebooks, 615 Second Avenue, Suite 260, Seattle, Washington 98104, 800/775-0817.

CONTENTS

ACKNOWLEDGMENTS

A warm thank you to Jerry Hughes, who first took me to Friday Harbor and Sucia Island in the 1950s in his little Bristol Bay fishing boat and forever associated the smell of gasoline and creosote, salt spray and boiled coffee, oyster stew and wet bathing suits, and the red branches of madrona trees and stars overhead with the San Juan Islands; to the ferry boat captain of the *Klickitat*, who gave permission for a 1970s wedding on board, a bouquet of honeysuckle, wild roses, and lupine picked from the roadside, at 8am on the route between Orcas and San Juan Islands; to potter Nancy Bingham, who provided a house and piles of veggies on rice to fuel this book the first time around; to Marian Hero, who accompanied me to B&Bs and is always willing to go down one more road; and to Charles Lathrop, who sailed me from port to port in his sloop *Skylark,* alongside pods of orca whales, and who, at dawn and dusk, jettisoned the kayaks off the deck to paddle into small bays and along shorelines; and lastly, to Mother Nature, who provided one of the most terrifying thunderstorms I've ever witnessed, in the middle of the night while we anchored off Thetis Island.

—*Jan Halliday*

ABOUT BEST PLACES GUIDEBOOKS

San Juan & Gulf Islands is part of the BEST PLACES® guidebook series, which means it's written by and for locals, who enjoy getting out and exploring the region. When making our recommendations, we seek out establishments of good quality and good value, places that are independently owned, run by lively individuals, touched with local history, or sparked by fun and interesting decor. Every place listed is recommended.

BEST PLACES® guidebooks, which have been published continuously since 1975, represent one of the most respected regional travel series in the country. Each guide is written completely independently: no advertisers, no sponsors, no favors. Our reviewers know their territory, work incognito, and seek out the very best a city or region has to offer. We provide tough, candid reports and describe the true strengths, foibles, and unique characteristics of each establishment listed.

Note: Readers are advised that the reviews in this edition are based on information available at press time and are subject to change. The editors welcome information conveyed by users of this book, as long as they have no financial connection with the establishment concerned. A report form is provided at the end of the book, and feedback is also welcome via email: books@SasquatchBooks.com.

HOW TO USE THIS BOOK

ACTIVITIES

Each town throughout this area has a variety of activities and attractions from which to choose. For quick and easy reference, we've created basic symbols to represent them, with full details immediately following. Watch for these symbols:

 Arts and crafts, galleries

 Beaches, swimming, beachcombing, water recreation

 Bicycling

 Boating, kayaking, other on-the-water activities

 Entertainment: movies, theater, concerts, performing arts, events

 Fishing (salt water and fresh)

 Food and drinks

 Historical sites, lighthouses

 Kid-friendly, family activities

 Local produce, farmers markets, farm products, organic foods

 Parks, wilderness areas, outdoor recreation, picnics

 Shops: clothing, books, antiques, souvenirs

 Views, scenic driving tours, other attractions

 Whale-watching, bird-watching, other wildlife viewing

RECOMMENDED RESTAURANTS
AND LODGINGS

At the end of each town section you'll find restaurants and lodgings recommended by our BEST PLACES®editors.

Rating System Establishments with stars have been rated on a scale of zero to four. Ratings are based on uniqueness, value, loyalty of local clientele, excellence of cooking, performance measured against goals, and professionalism of service.

(*no stars*)	Worth knowing about, if nearby
★	A good place
★★	Some wonderful qualities
★★★	Distinguished, many outstanding features
★★★★	The very best in the region

View Watch for this symbol throughout the book, indicating those restaurants and lodgings that feature a coastal or water view.

Price Range When prices range between two categories (for example, moderate to expensive), the lower one is given. Call ahead to verify.

$$$	Expensive. Indicates a tab of more than $80 for dinner for two, including wine (but not tip), and more than $100 for one night's lodging for two.
$$	Moderate. Falls between expensive and inexpensive.
$	Inexpensive. Indicates a tab of less than $35 for dinner, and less than $75 for lodgings for two.

Email and Web Site Addresses With the understanding that more people are using email and the World Wide Web to access information and to plan trips, BEST PLACES® has included email and Web site addresses of establishments, where available. Please note that the World Wide Web is a fluid and evolving medium, and that Web pages are often "under construction" or, as with all time-sensitive information in a guidebook such as this, may be no longer valid.

Checks and Credit Cards Most establishments that accept checks also require a major credit card for identification. Credit cards are abbreviated in this book as follows: American Express (AE); Diners Club (DC); Discover (DIS); MasterCard (MC); Visa (V).

Directions Throughout the book, basic directions are provided with each restaurant and lodging. Call ahead, however, to confirm hours and location.

Bed-and-Breakfasts Many B&Bs have a two-night minimum-stay requirement during the peak season, and several do not welcome children. Ask about a B&B's policies before you make your reservation.

Smoking Most establishments along the Olympic Peninsula do not permit smoking inside, although some lodgings have rooms reserved for smokers. Call ahead to verify an establishment's smoking policy.

Pets Most establishments do not allow pets; call ahead to verify, however, as some budget places do.

Index All restaurants, lodgings, town names, and major tourist attractions are listed alphabetically at the back of the book.

Reader Reports At the end of the book is a report form. We receive hundreds of reports from readers suggesting new places or agreeing or disagreeing with our assessments. They greatly help in our evaluations. We encourage you to respond.

SAN JUAN ISLANDS

SAN JUAN ISLANDS

Clustered between Vancouver Island and mainland British Columbia are 743 islands. Many are no more than a seagull perch; others support small communities accessible only by private boat or seaplane. The border between Canada and the United States divides this unique archipelago. Washington State Ferries services four islands in the United States: Lopez, Shaw, Orcas, and San Juan. These four are home to the bulk of the San Juan Islands' 10,000 full-time residents. Lopez, Orcas, and San Juan each has a well-stocked village center, as well as picturesque old general stores, historic hotels, and public beaches and parks dotting the rural landscape.

For years, most residents were farmers, fishermen, and storekeepers. Much of that began to change in the early 1970s, when well-educated young people began "dropping out" to live lightly in paradise. Although many of the Northwest's most well-to-do have had secret hideaways in the islands for years, people with pockets full of cash are the newest residents—building monumental homes on what was once humble rock and farmland.

Tucked into the "rain shadow" of the Olympic Mountains, the San Juans are a (mostly) blue-sky oasis in a land of clouds. Orcas, otters, seals, and numerous nesting birds, including a large population of bald eagles, hawks, and blue herons, make their homes here. Stands of tall firs, groves of red-barked madronas, grassy meadows, granite outcroppings, and hundreds of small protected bays and isolated coves lure tourists and new residents. The general rule of thumb: If you want to shop, eat, and watch whales, go to San Juan Island; if you want to hike and swim, go to Orcas Island; if you want to bike through farmland, go to Lopez. You can sample all three islands in about four very full days, including waiting in line for the ferry. We recommend a week.

If it's summer and you haven't nailed down a hotel reservation, you might think about taking the next boat back. Or call the B&B Hotline (21 members, 100 rooms) for room availability at 360/378-3030; their web site is updated hourly at www.san-juan-island.net.

Cars on Washington State Ferries only pay going westbound. If you plan to visit more than one island, arrange to go to the farthest island first (San Juan), and then work your way back east. An even better reason to leave the car behind: inter-island foot traffic is free, and you never wait in line.

GETTING THERE

Via Ferry. The most obvious and cost-effective way of getting to the San Juan Islands is via the Washington State Ferries. They run year-round (eight to nine trips daily) from Anacortes, 1½ hours north of Seattle, and two daily trips from Anacortes through the islands to Sidney, British Columbia, on Vancouver Island. Sidney is a half-hour north of Victoria (city bus service is available between Victoria and Sidney); for schedule and fare information for all routes (it changes each season), call 800/843-3779 or 206/464-6400.

Summer months, getting a car on a ferry out of Anacortes can be a long, dull, 3-hours-and-up wait; it's even longer at the Sidney dock. Bring a good book, walk on the crescent beach next to the Anacortes ferry landing while you wait—or park the car and walk on (for shuttle and parking info call 360/757-4433). All of the islands except Shaw have a few rental cars available (see individual islands); biking (you can rent bikes and mopeds on most islands) is another alternative.

Alternative Methods. The Victoria Clipper makes a twice-a-day trip from downtown Seattle to Friday Harbor on San Juan Island from mid-May through mid-October. One goes to Friday Harbor and on to Victoria. The other goes to Friday Harbor and

ACTIVITIES

 Island Events. March: Whale Festival, the Whale Museum, San Juan Island; 360/378-4710.

June: Farmers markets, all islands, June through October (or until the first big storm).

June: Artists' Studio Open House, each island. Call ahead for specific weekend; 360/468-3663.

July: Dixieland Jazz Festival, Friday Harbor, last weekend in July. The whole town swings with well-known jazz artists. For bands and ticket prices, call 360/378-5509. If you're planning to attend, reserve lodging far in advance (or stay on Orcas and walk over on the ferry for events); this has become a very popular festival.

August: Orcas Island Fly-In, Antique Airplane Show, at the airport. 360/376-2696.

Rosario Resort on Orcas Island. For Clipper information, call 800/888-2535.

You can also fly to the islands. Kenmore Air schedules daily float plane trips from Seattle's Lake Union to various destinations in the San Juan Islands. The airline offers attractive package deals too; 800/543-9595 or 206/364-5990. Harbor Airlines schedules commuter planes daily via Sea-Tac. Round-trip flights to San Juan, Lopez, and Orcas, 800/359-3220.

The San Juan Island Shuttle Express provides passenger-only ferry service from Bellingham to Eliza, Sinclair, Orcas, Lopez, and San Juan Islands, May to October; 360/671-1137. The San Juan Island Commuter 888/734-8180 offers daily service aboard a 49-passenger catamaran to islands not accessible by state ferry service, including Sucia (a marine park with 55-campsites), Stuart (campground and a wonderful hike to the Turn Point Lighthouse), Matia (a wildlife refuge), and Jones, among others. Best to check their web page at www.whales.com/ic.

Puget Sound Express provides passenger-only ferry service daily from Port Townsend to Friday Harbor, April to October. The captain takes the 3-hour scenic route, with whale-watching on the way back. Round-trip about $50; 360/385-5288.

If the brochure racks onboard the ferry or the San Juan Islands Visitor Information Service, 360/468-3663, didn't give you enough information, check out the local newspapers (The Journal and The Islands' Sounder) and posters listing current events. The Journal (580 Guard Street, Friday Harbor, 360/378-4191) publishes two all-island visitor guides winter and summer, with seasonal events listed.

August: San Juan County Fair, fairgrounds on San Juan Island's Argyle Street; 360/378-4310. Check out the Island Made and Grown booth and 4-H livestock auction.

September: The Lopez Wave (a.k.a the "Thank God They're Gone" celebration), Outdoor Pavilion, Lopez Village, Labor Day weekend.

ANACORTES

Anacortes, the gateway to the San Juans, is itself on an island: Fidalgo Island. Though most travelers rush through here on their way to the ferry, this town adorned with colorful, life-size cutouts of early pioneers is quietly becoming a place where it's worth it to slow down. For picnic or ferry food, try Geppetto's (3320 Commercial Avenue, 360/293-5033) for Italian take-out. Those with a little more time head to Gere-A-Deli (502 Commercial Avenue, 360/293-7383), a friendly hangout with good homemade food in an airy former Bank of Commerce building, or the Anacortes Brewhouse (320 Commercial Avenue, 360/293-2444), with its own brews and wood-oven pizzas. And don't forget the Calico Cupboard, offshoot of the well-known cafe and bakery in La Conner (901 Commercial Street, 360/293-7315).

If you need reading material for the ferry line, stop by Watermark Book Company (612 Commercial, 360/293-4277), loaded with interesting reads. Seafaring folks should poke around Marine Supply and Hardware (202 Commercial Avenue, 360/293-3014); established in 1913, it's packed to the rafters with basic and hard-to-find specialty marine items. And for the history of Fidalgo Island, visit the Anacortes Museum (1305 Eighth Street, 360/293-1915).

For those who plan to go kayaking in the islands, first stop by Eddyline Watersports Center (1019 Q Avenue, 360/299-2300); it is located at the Cap Sante Marina just before Anacortes (take a right on R Avenue off SR 20). Test-paddle a kayak in the harbor, then rent one for the weekend in the San Juans; reservations are necessary.

ACTIVITIES

Hike. A very pleasant hike that offers a sense of what the San Juans would be like if they were public land completely open to recreation is the Washington Park Loop, an easy, round-trip hike along a combination one-way road/walking path at Washington Park. The 3.5-mile loop is open to auto traffic, but cars are relatively rare, and in some places the single-track trail leaves the road and skirts the highly scenic cliffs and rocky beaches of Fidalgo Head.

Marina Facilities. Cap Sante Boat Haven (360/293-0694) a very nice facility managed by the Port of Anacortes, has extensive moorage, fuels, rest rooms, showers, laundry facilities, and nearby marine-supply stores. It's a primary starting point for many San Juan guided excursions, and boats and yachts often are turned over to renters here. Cap Sante is just east of downtown Anacortes.

Picnic. One of the best beachfront parks in the San Juan Islands isn't even technically *in* the San Juans. Washington Park, the 220-acre park on Fidalgo Head, just beyond the Anacortes Ferry Terminal, is one of the loveliest waterfront getaways in the Northwest. The day-use park has a pleasant beach and picnic area, and it offers wonderful views of Guemes Channel, the San Juans, and all the pleasure craft headed toward them. Grab a loaf of bread and a bottle of wine and while away the afternoon. It rarely disappoints.

RESTAURANTS

LA PETITE ☆☆

The Hulscher family, longtime owners of this restaurant at the Islands Inn motel, continues to deliver French-inspired food with a touch of Dutch. With only six entrees to choose from, quality is high. Try the lamb marinated in sambal or the popular pork tenderloin served with a mustard sauce. If chateaubriand is on the menu, order it; it's delicious. Soup, salad, and oven-fresh bread come with each meal. La Petite has an interesting dessert list, with plenty of options for chocolate lovers. A fixed-price Dutch breakfast is available for motel guests. *3401 Commercial Ave (at 34th), Anacortes, WA 98221; 360/293-4644; $$; full bar; AE, DC, DIS, MC, V; local checks only; breakfast every day, dinner Tues–Sun.*

JULIANNE'S GRILL (MAJESTIC HOTEL) ☆☆

It's the most elegant dining room in Anacortes, where diners are welcomed to a cathedral-ceilinged room filled with white tablecloths and tall-paned windows overlooking a garden and patio. The bistro has succeeded in combining the harvest of the Pacific Northwest with classic French cuisine and a Pacific Rim flair. At dinner, begin with grilled scallops served with a Thai peanut sauce. Mahi-mahi with an almond crust was fresh, moist and flavorful. There's also a Sunday champagne brunch, and live jazz Friday and Saturday nights in the pub. *419 Commercial Ave (between 4th and 5th), Anacortes, WA 98221; 360/299-9666; $$; full bar; AE, DIS, MC, V; checks OK; lunch, dinner every day.*

LODGINGS

CHANNEL HOUSE ☆☆

Just a mile and a half from the ferry dock, Dennis and Pat McIntyre's Channel House is a 1902 Victorian home designed by an Italian count. Each of the four antique-filled rooms has at least a peekaboo view of Guemes Channel and the San Juan Islands (best views are from the Canopy Room and the Island View Room). A cottage contains our two favorite rooms, however, each complete with a wood-burning fireplace and private whirlpool bath; the Victorian Rose has its own deck. There is a large hot tub out back, and the McIntyres serve cozy candlelit breakfasts (stuffed French toast is a specialty). Freshly baked oatmeal cookies and flavored coffee await guests returning from dinner. The McIntyres gladly accommodate guests who need breakfast early in order to catch a ferry to the San Juans, but the Channel House is worthy of a longer stay. *2902 Oakes Ave (at Dakota), Anacortes, WA 98221; 360/293-9382 or 800/238-4353; beds@sos.com; www.channel-house.com; $$; AE, DIS, MC, V; checks OK.*

THE MAJESTIC HOTEL ☆☆

Truly majestic, this 1889 hotel has been through a number of incarnations, but this is surely the grandest. It belongs on a bluff overlooking the Pacific, but provides a fine night's stay even in the middle of Anacortes. Every one of the 23 rooms is unique, all with English antiques; some have oversize tubs with skylights above, some have decks, others have VCRs, and a few have everything. The best rooms are the showy corner suites. On the second floor (the only smoking level) is a small library with a chess table. And up top, there's a cupola with a 360-degree view of Anacortes, Mount Baker, the Olympics, and the San Juans. There's no better perch in sight for a glass of wine at sunset. *419 Commercial Ave (between 4th and 5th), Anacortes, WA 98221; 360/293-3355 or 800/588-4780; $$$; AE, MC, V; checks OK.* &

SAN JUAN ISLAND

San Juan Island, the most populated in the archipelago, also supports the largest town in the islands, Friday Harbor. The town is named after Joe Friday, the Anglicized name of Joe Poalie, a Hawaiian native who was one of the island's first settlers. Joe first came to the Northwest from Hawaii in 1841 to work for the British Hudson's Bay Company at its Cowlitz Farm (on the trade route between the Columbia River and Puget Sound). Sometime after 1860, he moved to San Juan Island, grazed sheep, and lived in a cabin on what came to be known as Friday's Harbor (smoke from his chimney marked the harbor for early boatmen). Other Hawaiians, or "Kanakas," lived on the south end of the island (Kama Kamai, William Naukana, and William Nawana)—hence the name Kanaka Bay (between Lime Kiln Point and Cattle Point).

The ferry docks at Friday Harbor. Beginning at the ferry landing, the bustling little burg sprawls uphill, with a movie theater, performing arts center, whale museum, inns, and a multitude of shops, all within walking distance of the big boat. In recent years, new money, condominium development, and airport and dock expansion have upped the ante, and visitors storming around on mopeds (locals call these "road lice") make it all the more frantic in the summer. The only other development on the island is about 10 miles north at historic Roche Harbor Resort, which—always wildly popular with the boating set—also has caved in to condos. But if you visit San Juan in winter, you'll wonder what all the fuss is about; in terms of development, this is like Hawaii's Maui 30 years ago (though without the surf).

The two lighthouses on San Juan Island aren't open to the public, but they make a nice destination for a walk. The Cattle Point Lighthouse is easily accessible from the Department of Natural Resources land on the south end (at Cattle Point), or walk 2 miles from South Beach at American Camp at low tide. Take the path from Lime Kiln Point State Park to the 1919 lighthouse, a short walk with a great view of Haro Strait.

ACTIVITIES

Getting Around. You can spend half your weekend waiting for a ferry, or you can rent an island car or van from M & W Auto Rentals (725 Spring Street, 360/378-2886 or 800/323-6037). Cars can be taken off-island, but you gotta bring them back. Walk-ons can also take the bus around the island—the San Juan Shuttle—which picks up passengers at the ferry landing and stops at San Juan Vineyards, Lakedale Campground, the golf course, Whale Watch Park, San Juan County Park, Mitchell Bay, English Camp, and Roche Harbor for about $7

Old-timers say the streets of Friday Harbor once undulated with rabbits (a favorite pastime was crouching on the hood of a moving car and scooping rabbits into nets, like fishermen after salmon). But 20 years ago, a virus slowed down the rabbit population. Nonetheless, plenty remain, especially at American Camp. Watch for baby bunnies in the spring.

Wild turkeys are especially fond of English Camp. Turkeys can be intimidating if they're protecting a nesting hen. One woman's introduction to her new home on San Juan Island included a standoff with a large tom that ended when a neighbor walked her horse between the terrified newcomer and the big bird.

round-trip. Kids under 12 are free. You can buy a day pass for $10. You can also get to American Camp, South Beach, Cattle Point, and Cape San Juan with these folks, but you have to call them to arrange it; 360/378-8887. Taxi service is available too.

Another option is to buzz around on Susie's Mopeds, 360/378-5244, located one block from the ferry landing; or rent a Yamaha Razz Scooter—or better, a mountain bike—from Island Scooter & Bike Rentals, 360/378-8811, across from the ferry landing.

Parks. The largest parks on San Juan are actually two sites of San Juan Island National Historical Park: American Camp and English Camp, 19th-century military sites established when ownership of the island was under dispute. The conflict began in earnest with the infamous Pig War of 1859, so called because of the death by rifle of a Hudson's Bay Company pig rooting in the garden of an American settler. The "war" went on until 1872, with British and American troops and settlers jointly occupying the island until the dispute was settled in favor of the United States. English Camp, toward the island's north end, is wooded and secluded on lakelike Garrison Bay, while American Camp's 1,233 acres are mostly open prairie and beach, exposed to the windy Strait of Juan de Fuca and inhabited now only by thousands of brown rabbits. Allow a couple of hours at American Camp to go beachcombing on the windswept South Beach, the longest public beach in the islands. Summer weekends, costumed interpreters reenact camp-life scenes and talk about military life during the Civil War era; there are also guided "talks and walks."

Bird-watching. American Camp, on the island's south end, is a funnel for migrant birds; with strong winds come rare birds and many raptors. Birder and author Mark Lewis, in *Birding in the San Juan Islands,* says rare Eurasian larks are year-round residents, breeding only here and in the Hawaiian Islands. In early spring and summer, listen at the stone redoubt (where cannons were once mounted), a short walk from the interpretive center, for their sustained and complicated songs, composed of hundreds of notes.

Park in the lot overlooking American Camp's Old Town Lagoon and hike a short trail through a cedar and fir grove to Jakle's Lagoon, a soupy, brackish pond pooling behind a driftwood strand on Griffin Bay. There's good cover here to observe rafts of ducks, bald eagles, herons, and migrating seabirds. Extra bonus: North American river otters feed just offshore in the eelgrass meadows, chirping like birds.

The best shorebird and waterfowl site on San Juan is shallow False Bay, on the island's southwest side, which gets almost continuous use by migrating birds as they journey north and return south. In the winter, stop at Panorama Marsh on False Bay Road to see white trumpeter swans. Listen for the whistle in their wings when they lift off the water.

From the rocks at Cattle Point, from a little square of public land near the lighthouse on the southern tip of the island, watch for seabirds normally seen only from boats. You'll need binoculars to check out birds resting just offshore on barren Goose Island.

Get your hiking maps and other information on the historic English and American Camps at the National Park Service office (125 Spring Street, Friday Harbor, 360/378-2240), about two blocks from the ferry landing. A good reference for outdoorsy information.

Picnics. The broad lawn at English Camp, with its formal boxwood-hedge garden, white picket fence, maple trees, and guardhouse, cries for a wicker basket and red-and-white-checked cloth. Katrina's in Friday Harbor, 360/378-7290, fixes a hearty picnic basket with sandwiches on fresh-baked bread, along with her killer cookies. For a simple lunch, try homemade bagels and smoked chicken from Madelyn's, on A Street in Friday Harbor at the top of the ferry landing, 360/378-4545.

Felicity Milne, born in South Africa and a former San Francisco chef and caterer, offers morning and savory pastries and lovely breads baked with organic flour at Felicitations on Nichols Street, 360/378-1198. Everything is made from scratch. Local goat cheeses, raspberries, rhubarb, and other produce is used whenever possible.

Look for Alayne Sundberg's Quail Croft Farms goat cheese at the farmers market on Saturday mornings. Soft, mild, creamy cheese is made from the whole milk of Swiss Saanen goats raised on the farm; it is sold in 4- and 8-ounce cups—plain, or flavored with basil and garlic, tarragon and peppercorn, and other herbs.

You'll find picnic tables and fire pits along South Beach on the west side of American Camp (and parking is easy). For more privacy, hike the trails at the edge of the bluff to the north for picnics high above the beach or in intimate coves. Grandma's Cove on South Beach is a favorite. A caution: if you leave the trails to sit

"Diving is almost like being in outer space. You're in an unfamiliar medium, with an extra dimension to your movements. Everything you see is unfamiliar and exotic; it's like being in a different part of the universe."
—Alan Clews, diver

ISLAND CAMPING

For the best camping experience in the San Juans, pitch your tent in June or September; the weather's good, and your chances of landing a campsite are much better than in midsummer. State parks accept written reservations after January 1; no phone reservations at any state park on Orcas.

San Juan. The best campsites on San Juan are just beyond the whale-watching park at San Juan County Park, 360/378-2992. There are only 19 campsites at this pretty cove, so be sure to call for reservations in summer. Popular with bicyclists, Lakedale Resort (2627 Roche Harbor Road, Friday Harbor, WA 98250; 360/378-2350; www.lakedale.com) is a privately owned property of 84 acres with three lakes, fishing, swimming, boating, 120 campsites, and six beautifully appointed two-bedroom log cabins with fireplaces. Canoes, kayaks, paddleboats, and rowboats can be rented.

Orcas. The mammoth Moran State Park is a spectacular setting of 5,000 wooded acres with 30 miles of trails surrounding several lakes and Mount Constitution. With swimming, sailboarding, and canoeing, it's like summer camp (and just about as crowded). The 150 campsites fill up way before anyone is even

A 500-gallon aquarium next to Friday Harbor Seafoods (on the main pier) is filled with odd creatures fishermen bring in—such as box and decorator crabs, sculpins, and other fish. Bring the kids; touching is allowed.

somewhere out on the bare prairie, use extreme caution. The rabbits have perforated the ground with holes for the past 100 years, and it's easy to sprain or break an ankle in a giddy search for the perfect picnic spot.

A great spot, aptly named Picnic Beach, is on Griffin Bay in American Camp. Park in the lot and walk onto the good stretch of pebble beach for lunch on a log. Fires are allowed here (5 feet below the driftwood line)—good news for oyster lovers who like to grill them in the shell.

Picnic tables under a shed roof above the Port of Friday Harbor overlook the busy marina—a very pretty spot to have lunch. You can also take your lunch out on the public wharf in front of Friday Harbor. Our personal favorite: rent a kayak or rowboat, paddle out of the way of ship traffic, and picnic in the boat.

 Diving. The best diving in the archipelago (some claim it's the best cold-water diving in the world) can be had off *thinking of summer. Reserve early by writing to Moran State Park anytime after January 1 (Star Route Box 22, Eastsound, WA 98245; 360/376-2326). Obstruction Pass Marine State Park, at the south tip of the island, is designed primarily for boaters. This remote campground (accessible only by boat or on foot) has only 9 sites, no running water, and a half-mile hike to the beach. We like it for these reasons. No fees, sites are on a first-come, first-get basis; 360/468-3663.*

Shaw. The best bet for a campsite on Shaw is, oddly enough, at one of the smallest campgrounds in the islands. The Shaw Island State Park, at the south end of the island, has only 12 sites. No reservations.

Lopez. Spencer Spit State Park is a tree-covered slope that leads down to a sandy spit almost touching the shore of Frost Island. Of the 50 campsites, the nicest are the 8 walk-ins on the beach, with barbecues and picnic tables. Reservations can be made 11 months in advance; 800/452-5687; info 360/468-2251. Odlin County Park, only 1¾ miles from the ferry landing, has 30 sites ($10) scattered along a small beach and facing Shaw Island; 360/468-2496.

August, when islanders are taking their animals to and from the San Juan County Fair, is a great time to ride the ferry with your children.

In 1903 a University of Washington entomology professor was among the researchers studying biology on San Juan Island. He dubbed the site "the Bug Station." By 1922 it had evolved into the University of Washington Friday Harbor Laboratories, on University Road, where scientists and graduate students from all over the world conduct zoology, botany, oceanography, and fisheries studies. The lab, visible from Friday Harbor's waterfront and surrounded by woods, is deluged with requests to visit, but, unfortunately, is unable to offer tours.

San Juan Island. Tom Hemphill, who's been scuba diving in the San Juans since 1967, names these three favorites: the submerged, 120-foot vertical wall covered with purple, scarlet, and white sea anemones, off Turn Island; the challenging currents, diverse fish, and carpet of anemones and sponges south of Cattle Point; and the undersea caves and canyons—home to shy octopi and wolf eels—off Bell Island (between Shaw and Orcas Islands). Check with Emerald Seas Aquatics (180 First Street, Friday Harbor, 360/378-2772) for charters, rentals, and classes.

Fresh Seafood. The Oyster Bar Restaurant in New York's Grand Central Station buys Westcott Bay Sea Farm's succulent gourmet oysters, cultivated in the pristine waters of Westcott Bay on San Juan Island's northwest end (4071 Westcott Drive, 360/378-2489). Look for signs on Roche Harbor Road pointing down a dirt road (full of potholes) and follow it to the shack at the end. They grow the pretty Belon European flat and

Take a look at
Annie Adams's
chalk pastels of
Fiesta and other
wares at her Funk
& Junk secondhand
store. Winters, she
peruses the country
for cool stuff for
her store and
teaches art at
Skagit Valley Com-
munity College's
branch on San Juan
Island.

Launch your boat
and fish year-round
for bass and trout
at Egg and Sports-
man Lakes. Get
maps, licenses, and
gear at Friday Har-
bor Hardware &
Marine,
360/378-4622.

the sweet and mildly salty Westcott Bay, a cross between Japan's Miyagi and Kumamoto oysters. These are grown mostly for the restaurant trade. The farm also seeds its beach with Manila clams. You select oysters or clams out of cold-water tubs near the dock. But for the Real Oyster Experience, show up at low tide and pick oysters off the beach at Westcott Bay for $2 a pound, a real deal. Westcott Bay Sea Farm provides gloves and leaky rubber boots, in case you forgot yours. There's a wash table with hose and scrubbing things to clean off the oysters. Several times each summer, Westcott offers a U-pick special for as low as 25 cents an oyster. The farm also ships fresh oysters by overnight mail.

Friday Harbor Seafoods, 360/378-5779, in the shack on the 80-foot barge moored to the main pier, sells freshly caught local seafood, including live Dungeness crab, spot prawns, singing scallops, oysters, and clams, all held in four huge pens on the deck. They'll cook and clean your crab for you, but you have to crack it. Crab, shrimp, and prawn cocktails and smoked salmon are great, too—all you need is a loaf of bread for a feast. Dock space is available alongside for pleasure boaters stopping to buy fish. Make up your own box lunch—with a whole crab and all the fixings, sandwiches, and chips. Seafood platters with fresh oysters, clams, prawns, and crab can be delivered to your boat (yes, even all the way across to Roche Harbor).

Shopping. As the island draws more monied visitors and residents, so do its shops. Old buildings and houses have been turned into cute little shops that change ownership and flavor often. Shopping begins at the ferry landing and continues for about four square blocks. That's it. It's all fun to look at, with a refreshing dearth of tacky souvenirs. Among our favorite stops are King's Marine for outdoorwear, island books, maps, and marine supplies; Griffin Bay Books for its eclectic collection and friendly pup sprawled across the doorway; and Arctic Raven Gallery, 360/378-3433, which carries authentic Coast Salish Indian fine art (wood carvings, etched glass, sculpture, and prints) from around the Puget Sound region.

Island Crafts. A small selection of hand-spun island yarns (as well as wool from small island sheep farms), sweaters, shawls, and handmade buttons is at Island Knits & Notions (30 First Street S, Friday Harbor, 360/378-4128). Visit

AnniKin Galleries (165 First Street, Friday Harbor, 360/378-7286) for Yates Lansing's driftwood furniture; Moussa Green's "crying man" fountains (tears pour out of his eyes and onto his tongue, and puddle at his feet); Yvonne Buij's silver, stone, and glass jewelry (including work by local children); and owner Anne Sheridan's hand-tinted images taken with her 4x5 camera.

The best fine art in the archipelago that we've seen is at Waterworks Gallery (315 Spring Street, Friday Harbor, 360/378-3060). Year-round, the work of 33 regional artists the owner considers the best in their media are represented here. She really separates the wheat from the chaff, artwise.

Fishing. Gear and licenses for saltwater fishing, as well as information about seasons, techniques, and limits for salmon, shellfish, and bottom fish, all are available at Friday Harbor Hardware & Marine (270 Spring Street, 360/378-4622), King's Marine (110 Spring Street, 360/378-4593), Duke's Sporting Goods (280 Spring Street, 360/378-6271), and Roche Harbor Grocery (on the dock, 360/378-5562). You can buy crab bait and frozen and live bait, as well as rent gear, at Friday Harbor Seafoods, on the main pier, 360/378-5779.

Marinas. San Juan Island's Port of Friday Harbor, 360/378-2688, operates a large, full-service marina at the foot of the islands' largest town. With nearly 464 slips (100 of which are for guests), commercial charters, live-aboards, a seafood shop, purse seiners and gillnetters, and the constant flow of boats and boaters, the marina is like a floating village itself. Seaplanes and ferries come in and out of the harbor daily, so it's an ideal spot to pick up or drop off crew. It's also the place to clear U.S. Customs, refuel, resupply, pump out, shower, make repairs, and perform all those other necessary chores before heading out to more idyllic anchorages.

All boaters remember their first visit to Roche Harbor, whether it was spotting the trellised gardens in front of the historic, sagging Hotel de Haro (built in 1886), admiring the little white church on the madrona- and evergreen-covered hill, or anchoring out in the bay because the Roche Harbor Resort & Marina, 800/451-8910, was crammed with partying boaters. Located on the island's north end, Roche may be miles from Friday Harbor, but, especially in the summer, it's a hubbub of resort

San Juan Coffee Roasting Company roasts 19 kinds of coffee and sells it wholesale, mail-order, and at its retail shop at 18 Cannery Landing, Friday Harbor, 360/378-4443. Also available: freshly brewed espresso, brewing equipment, and fine chocolates.

and boating activity. Amenities include groceries, fuel, laundry service, showers, U.S. Customs, guided kayak tours, boat rentals, outdoor heated pool, volleyball and tennis courts, three restaurants, one- to three-bedroom condos, cottages, and the pleasure of visiting one of the state's oldest resorts.

Snug Harbor Resort in Mitchell Bay (2371 Mitchell Bay Road, 360/378-4762), on the island's west side, handles boats under 60 feet and has a small general store and showers, kayak rentals, whale-watching charters, and cabins for rent. Twelve-, fourteen-, and sixteen-foot aluminum skiffs equipped with Nissan outboard motors cost $60 for a half day and rental includes life jackets, flares, and oars. The protected bay itself is fine to explore, but you can zip up narrow and rocky Mosquito Pass to Roche Harbor and poke around offshore Henry and Pearl Islands.

Farm and Garden. Visit the Friday Harbor farmers' market for fresh produce, berries, baked goods—great stuff for picnics—Saturdays throughout the summer, on the County Courthouse parking lot.

Michelle and Brian Lambright own the popular Giannangelo Farms (5500 Limestone Point Road, 360/378-4218), an organic garden carved out of 16 acres of woods on the island's north end. Salad greens, vegetables, fresh garlic, and flowers are for sale, as well as dried herbs, herbed and raspberry vinegars, teas, and floral and garlic wreaths (mail-order catalog available). A berry field and an apple orchard have been planted for future U-pickers. Open March to October.

Colleen Howe's large English cottage garden spills over with old-world roses and other perennials (6451 Mitchell Bay Road, 360/378-2309). Outside the tall fence that surrounds the garden, she's testing deer-proof plants: the hungry critters don't like lavender, purple sage, 40 varieties of heather, ornamental grasses, or asters. All are for sale, propagated from cuttings. Visitors may walk through the garden 11am to 5pm weekends from April to mid-October. Look for the Lombardy poplars and pink farmhouse on 20 acres.

You can't pick the flowers, but check out the pretty gardens surrounded by a white picket fence in front of the Hotel de Haro (named after the Haro Strait, which was named after a Spanish explorer) in Roche Harbor.

A HOME AWAY FROM HOME?

Rent a house or cabin, and see what it's like to be an island resident. Cherie L. Lindholm Real Estate, 360/376-2204, handles vacation rentals on Orcas. The list is not huge, mind you, but a waterfront cabin wouldn't be a bad way to spend a week or two. Re/Max San Juan Island, 800/992-1904 or 360/378-5060, handles most of the rental properties on San Juan Island (although they are more pricey than those on Orcas). Barbara Pickering 360/468-3401 or 360/468-3368, manages vacation rentals on Lopez.

Caution: Most of the land and many local roads on San Juan are privately owned. Owners will prosecute trespassers. Also, the fine for bikers riding two abreast on a roadway—or similar traffic infractions—is $50.

The McEnerys (call first, 360/378-4852) sell honey flavored with raspberry, mint, gooseberry, blackberry, and madrona. The flavored honeys come in tiny little jars you can stick in your luggage, and plain honey comes in l-pound jars. Look for them at farmers market on Saturdays.

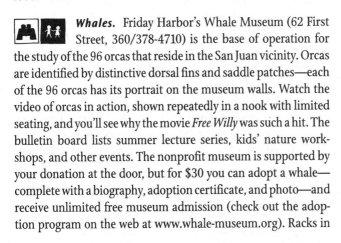

Brew Pub. Oren Combs brews full-grain beer—ales, bitters, Hefeweizen, porters, and lagers—in the stainless steel tanks for the San Juan Brewing Company adjoining the Front Street Ale House (1 Front Street, Friday Harbor, 360/378-2337). Twelve beers are on tap or in bottles in the Ale House, along with potpies, bangers and mash, and other English pub food.

Whales. Friday Harbor's Whale Museum (62 First Street, 360/378-4710) is the base of operation for the study of the 96 orcas that reside in the San Juan vicinity. Orcas are identified by distinctive dorsal fins and saddle patches—each of the 96 orcas has its portrait on the museum walls. Watch the video of orcas in action, shown repeatedly in a nook with limited seating, and you'll see why the movie *Free Willy* was such a hit. The bulletin board lists summer lecture series, kids' nature workshops, and other events. The nonprofit museum is supported by your donation at the door, but for $30 you can adopt a whale—complete with a biography, adoption certificate, and photo—and receive unlimited free museum admission (check out the adoption program on the web at www.whale-museum.org). Racks in the vestibule are crammed with whale-watching charter brochures. Open daily in summer.

Don't miss the Whale Museum Store next door (61 First Street, Friday Harbor, 360/378-4710), where the T-shirts are fabulous—from celestial whales to Northwest Coast Indian designs. The store also offers stirring whale videos and a fine selection of adult and children's books about things ecologic. Also look here for *Orcas' Greatest Hits*, Interspecies Communication's recording of musicians jamming with the modulated whistles and pulsed clicks of whale song. The musicians invited the orca pods to sing with them by transmitting live music into the water and then recording the cetacean responses on mikes dangling over the side of the boat.

The first whale-watching park established in the nation is at Lime Kiln Point State Park, just south of San Juan County Park on Lighthouse Road. A research station since 1983, it has underwater microphones that eavesdrop on unsuspecting orcas. The killer whales pass by regularly, especially in summer months. The grassy slopes, with their wild orange poppies and westerly view toward Vancouver Island, are diversion enough when the whales aren't around. You can get there on the bus from Friday Harbor; 360/378-8887.

Best Vacation Buy. North Cascades Institute offers year-round weekend classes throughout Washington State—many in the San Juan Islands. Classes include a four-day naturalist cruise aboard the 65-foot *Snow Goose* with ecologist Dr. Bert Webber; two nights with Peter Capan, observing whales and porpoises; and sessions on coastal geology, birds and wildflowers, watercolor painting, and field journal illustration. Other "oh, wow!" classes have been Raven Ecology and Mythology and Marine Mammals of Puget Sound. Most classes cost less than $200 (including lodging). In our opinion, this is the best bargain in the islands. Write or call for their current catalog: 2105 State Route 20, Sedro Woolley, WA 98284-9394, 360/856-5700, ext. 209.

Hiking. Begin on the marked trail from English Camp's parking lot, walk ¼ mile through an alder grove, cross the blacktop road, and follow the trail up 650-foot Mount Young. It's steep, but only another ¼ mile to the first viewpoint. The vista of the Olympic Mountains, Vancouver Island, Gulf Islands, and San Juan's northwest bays is astounding (and interpreted on a sign). You'll notice an unmarked trail continuing up; bear right, and go all the way to the top—to what feels like hallowed ground: bare rock carpeted with fluorescent green moss, lichens, and stonecrop, rimmed by firs.

Pat Flores quit her job and moved to Friday Harbor after she saw a postcard of the area while sorting mail in a San Francisco post office.

Another viewpoint is at American Camp's 290-foot Mount Finlayson. Hike through what islanders call "the enchanted forest" up a gentle slope breaking into prairie where, on a clear day, you can see major Cascade peaks. A mile-long self-guided interpretive trail begins at the Exhibit Center at American Camp (the first dirt road past the American Camp sign on Cattle Point Road). The trail loops around the old army camp, now nothing more than a huge picket fence around a grassy field, an old farmhouse, and former laundress's quarters. Go through the gate to a group of stones in the redoubt, where cannons were once mounted. From this point you can hike across the grassy, treeless prairie to Grandma's Cove and follow a trail along the bluff the length of South Beach, or circle back to the parking lot. Watch for terns, gulls, plovers, turnstones, yellowlegs, and bald eagles. You may also see orcas offshore.

Yellow Island's 10 acres, about 20 minutes from San Juan Island by private boat, are blanketed with chocolate lilies, buttercups, Indian paintbrush, and white fawn lilies from March to early June, followed by blue camas. Open meadows are protected by The Nature Conservancy, and visits are limited to groups smaller than six, except by permission (call the Seattle office, 206/343-4344). You must stay on marked trails to protect the flowers. Picnicking, smoking, fires, camping, and pets are prohibited. No peeing, either! Friendly island stewards live in half-century-old log cabins.

Island History. It's a pretty spot: white-steepled Valley Church stands next to a short road on a rise overlooking farmland. First named Cemetery Road because two graveyards, Catholic and Protestant, flank it, the road was renamed Madden Lane a few years ago. The name change confounded a hearse driver from the mainland who arrived hours late with the deceased, the driver apologizing profusely because he'd driven all over the island trying to find Cemetery Road. "That's OK," the widow assured him, "my husband would have loved the ride."

You won't get lost if you pick up the self-guided historic landmark brochure for a walking tour of Friday Harbor, the commercial and political hub of the islands since the 1890s. A brief paragraph about each of 32 sites explains architecture that is common in these small burgs—fishermen, farmers, loggers, and traders built what they could afford. The oldest house dates to 1860, once part of the barracks at American Camp. At the turn of the century, four wharves served the waterfront—it wasn't unusual to see sheep or turkeys being herded down Spring Street toward the docks. Keep that in mind when you begin about a block from the ferry landing and work your way up to James King's Farmhouse, built in the early 1890s and now the San Juan Historical Museum (405 Price Street, 360/378-3949). The homestead includes a farmhouse, carriage house, stone root cellar, the original milk house, a barn filled with old farm equipment, and San Juan County's first jail (moved here).

Etta Lightheart Egeland, with others, founded this museum, establishing it first in a log cabin from the island's west side where she danced as a girl. Egeland was delivered by a Native American midwife on San Juan Island, where her mother was also born. She grew up at the turn of the century surrounded by the "whales, sea life, and abundance of the earth," she says. A typical island resident, though she scandalized her family when she bobbed her hair in Roaring '20s style, Egeland summered in Victoria; filleted fish in a cannery at 14; washed dishes at the Tourists Hotel; worked in the pea cannery, the island schools, and the University of Washington lab kitchen; married at 17; lost her young son to polio; and, in later years, managed Friday Harbor's liquor store. With her passionate interest in island history, Egeland has been the steward of islanders' family treasures for more than 50 years. At this writing, Etta is 102 years old and works at the museum as a docent a couple of days a week.

Community Theater. Friday Harbor's community theater is just that: community. Built with donations and staffed mostly by volunteers, the little 285-seat theater stages darn good high school and local performances—some of them locally written—as well as chamber and choral music, and traveling shows. Check the box office or local paper for dates (100 Second Street, Friday Harbor, 360/378-3210).

RESTAURANTS

DUCK SOUP INN ☆☆

Richard and Gretchen Allison are committed to a kitchen with an ambitious reach using local seafoods and seasonal ingredients, and they've succeeded admirably. The wood-paneled dining room, with its stone fireplace, wooden booths, and high windows, is a charmer. The menu is limited to house specialties—succulent sautéed prawns in wild blackberry sauce, applewood-smoked Westcott Bay oysters, and grilled fresh fish. House-baked bread served with tangy anchovy paste (and butter), a small bowl of perfectly seasoned soup, and a large green salad accompany the ample portions. No wonder there's little room left for dessert. *3090 Roche Harbor Rd, Friday Harbor, WA 98250; 360/378-4878; $$; beer and wine; DIS, MC, V; checks OK; dinner Wed–Sun (closed in winter).*

KATRINA'S ☆

Kate Stone has moved her one-woman culinary show from the back of a secondhand store to an airy Victorian with more space for diners. You can sit at the counter and watch this dynamo cook or lose yourself in one of the rooms on the first floor (all orders are taken at the counter before you sit down). Kate's doing more seafood now, but by and large look for the same rotating-menu format of simple sensations chalked on the blackboard: her signature spinach-cheese pie and green salad with toasted hazelnuts and garlicky blue cheese dressing are standouts. Breads are homemade, and so are desserts, which favor fruit cobblers and heaping pieces of pie; Kate's sweetest specialty: decorated birthday cakes. Been waiting too long? Just tell the cook and she'll bring it to the table herself. Check out the breezy deck and live music on weekends. *135 2nd St (corner of West, downtown), Friday Harbor, WA 98250; 360/378-7290; $; beer and wine; MC, V; checks OK; lunch, early dinner Mon–Fri.*

Pool, darts, ladies' nights, beer, wine, greasy burgers, fries, hot dogs, live music some nights—just like the good old days—at Herb's Tavern (80 First Street S, 360/378-9106), a Friday Harbor institution since the 1940s.

Island musicians, poets, and artists perform in local restaurants, often at the Springtree Cafe (310-C Spring Street, Friday Harbor, 360/378-4848).

THE PLACE NEXT TO
THE SAN JUAN FERRY CAFE ☆

 Behind the unassuming name and the viewy waterside location that typically guarantees mediocrity is this striving concern, garnering much praise from locals. Chef/owner Steven Anderson features a rotating world of cuisines, focusing on fish and shellfish, from BC king salmon to Westcott Bay oysters. On a recent visit we enjoyed a fillet of salmon in a gingery citrus sauce, and a plate of black bean ravioli topped with tiger prawns in a buttery glaze. Servers know exactly how much time you have if your boat is in sight: with luck, enough time to savor the sumptuous crème caramel. *1 Spring St (on the water, at the foot of Spring St), Friday Harbor, WA 98250; 360/378-8707; $$; beer and wine; MC, V; checks OK; dinner every day (open through the winter, but call for hours).*

SPRINGTREE CAFE ☆

Chef/owner Steven Anderson bought the Springtree Cafe last year and garners as much praise for his effort here as at The Place Next to the San Juan Ferry Cafe (see review above). Decor has remained simple—no tablecloths, plain wooden tables graced by a few fresh flowers, some photographs on the walls. But the menu, emphasizing seafood, organics, and local produce, is anything but simple. There's almost always a grilled salmon preparation on the menu, and flavors lean toward Pacific Rim (that's Asian, folks) rather than European. There's outdoor dining under the elm tree on the patio, weather permitting. *310 Spring St (nearly hidden by the elm tree out front), Friday Harbor, WA 98250; 360/378-4848; $$; beer and wine; MC, V; local checks only; dinner every day (closed off-season, call first).*

LODGINGS

DUFFY HOUSE ☆

 This 1920s farmhouse looking out upon Griffin Bay and the Olympics beyond displays an architectural style (Tudor) that's rare in the islands, on a splendid, isolated site. Decorated with antiques and accented with classic mahogany trim, Duffy House offers five comfy guest rooms, all of which have private baths. The sunken living room sports a large fireplace and a bounty of information about the islands. Even neophyte bird-watchers won't be able to miss the bald eagles here; they nest just across the street, near the trail to the beach. *760 Pear Point Rd (take Argyle Rd south from town to Pear Point Rd), Friday Harbor, WA 98250; 800/972-2089 or 360/378-5604; duffyhouse@rockisland.com; www.san-juan.net/duffyhouse; $$; MC, V; checks OK.*

FRIDAY HARBOR HOUSE

 Some shudder at the sore-thumb architecture of San Juan Island's most expensive inn, a sister property of the Inn at Langley on Whidbey Island. Others consider this stylish urban outpost a welcome relief from Victorian B&Bs. Regardless, the interior is a bastion of spare and soothing serenity, a mood abetted by the professional management of the place. Each of the 20 rooms is decorated in muted tones, lending a contemporary feel, with gas fireplaces and (noisy) Jacuzzis positioned to absorb both the warmth from the fireplace and the harbor view. Some rooms have tiny standing-room-only balconies (we wonder what the architect was thinking), but not all offer a full waterfront view. Breakfast is continental, with delicious hot scones.

The dining room, with its knockout harbor view, maintains the spartan cool of the rest of the inn, but warms up considerably under the influence of chef Laurie Paul's expert cooking. Service is efficient. *130 West St (from ferry, left on Spring, right on 1st, right on West), PO Box 1385, Friday Harbor, WA 98250; 360/378-8455; fhhouse@rockisland.com; www.fridayharborhouse.com; $$$; full bar; AE, MC, V; checks OK; dinner every day (closed Tues–Wed in winter).*

FRIDAY'S HISTORICAL INN ☆

The former Elite Hotel is living up to its old name. Innkeepers Debbie and Steve Demarest took this longtime bunkhouse and gave it a completely new life. Eleven rooms are decorated in rich colors of wine, water, and wings. The best room in the place is unquestionably the third-floor

Okay, you really blew it and forgot to make a reservation, or you are on a budget and spending most of your dough on whale watching. Stay at The Orca Inn, the San Juan Island's only budget motel—76 rooms begin at $49 (winter rates) and include rolls and coffee, cable TV, and free shuttle to the ferry (it's only about four blocks away). 770 Mullis Street, 888/541-ORCA.

Tennis courts and a running track are free at Friday Harbor's high school (45 Blair Avenue, summers only).

perch with its own deck (and water view), kitchen, double shower, and Jacuzzi. Heated floors in the bathrooms and occasional fresh-baked cookies are just two of the thoughtful touches; however, the inn is right in the middle of town and not always the quietest retreat. *35 1st St. (2 blocks up from the ferry on 1st St), PO Box 2023, Friday Harbor, WA 98250; 800/352-2632 or 360/378-5848; fridays@friday-harbor.com; www.friday-harbor.com; $$; MC,V; checks OK.*

HARRISON HOUSE SUITES

 This crisply renovated Craftsman inn, just up the hill from downtown Friday Harbor and run by the effusive Farhad Ghatan, features five impressive suites: all with kitchens and private baths, four with decks, three with whirlpool tubs, and three with fireplaces (one wood-burning). It's modern and angular, and view rooms overlook the whole scenic sweep of Friday Harbor. There's a pretty water garden, plus flower, fruit, and vegetable gardens for use of the guests— the only place we've seen in the islands where you can pick your own garden salad and toss it in your own kitchen. All this and it's underpriced, for the region—great for families and/or groups of couples. Complimentary fresh-baked breads are served each evening; each morning Ghatan delivers fresh scones. Ghatan also runs a little cafe on the premises—for guests only—for private dinners, parties, and catered events. *235 C St (2 blocks from downtown, at Harrison St), Friday Harbor, WA 98250; 800/407-7933 or 360/378-3587; hhsuites@rockisland.com; www.san-juan-lodging.com; $$; AE, DIS, MC, V; checks OK.*

HIGHLAND INN

 Innkeeper of note Helen King sold her deservedly famous 12-room Babbling Brook Inn in Santa Cruz a few years ago, packed it up, and moved to the west side of San Juan Island. There she built the inn of her dreams: just two lovely suites, one at each end of her house, both with views of the Olympic Mountains, Victoria, and Haro Strait from the 88-foot-long deck. Licensed for just two couples a night (no children), the Highland Inn is everything you could ask for—in both privacy and hospitality. Suites are huge, with sitting rooms and wood-burning (!) fireplaces and marble bathrooms—each with its own whirlpool tub for two and steam-cabinet shower. One suite is elegantly furnished in black and beige with English antiques; the other is decorated in country French—warm yellows and blues and pine furniture. Guests may use the whirlpool bath on the deck, but don't bother with the noisy jets—they might drown out the sighing of orca whales that feed on migrating salmon in Haro Strait just offshore (the inn is less than 1 mile south of Lime Kiln Point State Park, one of the best places in the islands to watch the whales). Guests share a common dining room between the two suites, but you can have a generous breakfast served in your suite or on the deck. *PO Box 135 (call for directions), Friday Harbor, WA 98250; 888/400-9850 or 360/378-9450; helen@highlandinn.com; www.highlandinn. com; $$$; AE, MC, V; checks OK.*

LONESOME COVE RESORT

 Back in 1945, Roy and Neva Durhack sailed their 35-foot yacht here from the Hawaiian Islands. They were getting ready to sail it around the world, but once they saw Lonesome Cove their wanderlust subsided. They're not here anymore—the (Cellular One) McCaw brothers of Seattle bought the place and reduced the wooded acreage from 75 to 10 acres— but the resort remains a pretty spot. The six immaculate little cabins set among trees at the water's edge, the manicured lawns, and the domesticated deer that wander the woods make the place a favorite for lighthearted honeymooners. The sunsets are spectacular, and there's a fine view of nearby Spieden Island. Cabins have a five-night minimum stay in June and July (two nights at other times). No pets—too many baby ducks around. *416 Lonesome Cove Rd (take Roche Harbor Rd 9 miles north to Lonesome Cove Rd), Friday Harbor, WA 98250; 360/378-4477; $$; MC, V; checks OK.*

OLYMPIC LIGHTS

 As you approach this isolated bed-and-breakfast, you may recall the movie *Days of Heaven:* the tall Victorian farmhouse sits lonely as a lighthouse in a sea of open meadow.

The renovated interior is more modern and elegant: four upstairs rooms and one down, all with queen beds and private baths (being installed at this writing), are furnished with white wicker and bathed in sunlight. You must remove your shoes to tread the off-white pile carpet. The panorama of Olympic Mountains and Strait of Juan de Fuca from the south rooms adds to the effect. Breakfast includes fresh eggs from the resident hens; the owners also have five cats who roam downstairs. *4531-A Cattle Point Rd (take Argyle Ave out of Friday Harbor to Cattle Point Rd), Friday Harbor, WA 98250; 360/378-3186; www.san-juan.net/olympiclights; $$; no credit cards; checks OK.*

ROCHE HARBOR RESORT

 When you walk out of the stately old ivy-clad Hotel de Haro at Roche Harbor and gaze out at the trellised, cobblestoned waterfront and yacht-crammed bay, you might forget all about the creaky, uneven floorboards, the piecework wallpaper, the sparse furnishings. This faded gem evolved from the company town that John McMillin built a century ago for his lime quarry (lime from this quarry sweetened the huge salt marsh that was filled in and became the tulip fields of the Skagit Valley). It was once the largest such quarry west of the Mississippi. At this writing, four new luxury suites (the McMillin Suites) are opening in McM's old house, which also houses the resort's largest restaurant. Suites have killer views, large claw-foot soaking tubs, big beds, and room service. The old hotel has seen some renovation since Teddy Roosevelt visited, but not so you'd notice. Here are single rooms with shared baths and four suites with private baths. We remember entering this harbor for the first time, when the old hotel was still surrounded with deep green forests and wooden boats tied up at the dock—a mysterious, beautiful spot. That's all changed with rampant condo and residential development. Still, for newcomers, the 112-year-old resort has a terrific view and pretty gardens, plus a few nicely renovated cottages and condos. Between strolling the gardens, swimming, tennis, and visiting the mausoleum (really), there's plenty to do at Roche Harbor. *PO Box 4001 (on the waterfront),*

Roche Harbor, WA 98250; 800/451-8910 or 360/378-2155; roche@rocheharbor; www.rocheharbor.com; $$$; AE, MC, V; checks OK.

TOWER HOUSE B&B

Everything was pleasing to us—the story of how this lovely Queen Anne Victorian was barged to San Juan Island from Victoria, BC; the antiques; the linens; the view from the front porch, which includes a lovely weathered barn, a sweep of fields against the evergreens, and False Bay in the distance; and the two unusual first-floor rooms. We chose the relatively inexpensive Sun Room with its own sunny porch and entry because the Tower Room, with its stained glass windows, antiques, and window seat looking west, was booked by honeymooners. And the breakfast! Catering especially to vegetarians, breakfast was ample, fresh, and fat free. Chris and Joe Luma may be the only B&B hosts in the northern hemisphere who have no qualms about serving quinoa, a protein-rich South American grain, for breakfast—along with such delights as Moroccan pie, polenta, apricot-orange couscous, hot stuffed tomatoes, lemon popovers, and fresh pears. If you aren't a vegetarian already, you may change your mind. Meals are also prepared for those with challenging special needs (vegan, gluten-free, macrobiotic, diabetic). Chris and Joe urge guests to walk—whether it be a short hike to the top of the hill, 1 mile to the Island Church and Cemetery, or 3 miles to town. Or walk one way and they'll get you back to where you started (pickup service from the ferry, too). *1230 Little Rd, Friday Harbor, WA 98250; 800/858-4276 or 360/378-5464; towerhouse@ san-juan-island.com; www.san-juan-island.com; $$; MC, V; checks OK.*

TRUMPETER INN

Trumpeter Inn is a contemporary house located amid farmland about 2 miles outside Friday Harbor. The pastoral setting is soothing, as are the updated guest rooms decorated in soft pastels, ivories, or dark plaids. All rooms have a king- or queen-size bed with crisp cotton sheets and down comforters; five rooms have private baths; two have gas fireplaces and private decks. A hot tub is a short pad down the garden path; robes and slippers are provided. We prefer the Bay Laurel Room, a second-floor corner room with fireplace, with a great view of the surrounding meadows and the Olympics in the distance. Bobbie and Don Wiesner cook breakfast together: always fresh fruit and a spread that might include a walnut torte, quiche, or baked apple french toast and fresh-baked bread. Guests may eat whenever they wish. You may even glimpse the trumpeter swans for whom the inn is named if you visit in winter. Leave your car behind; owners can pick up guests from the ferry. *318 Trumpeter Way (from Friday Harbor, follow Spring St, which runs into San Juan Valley Rd), Friday Harbor, WA 98250; 800/826-7926 or 360/378-3884; www.trumpeterinn.com; $$; AE, DIS, MC, V; checks OK.*

WHARFSIDE BED & BREAKFAST ☆

If nothing lulls you to sleep like the gentle lap of the waves, the Wharfside's the B&B for you. It's this region's first realization of the European tradition of floating inns. Two guest rooms on the 60-foot sailboat *Jacquelyn* are both very nicely finished, and full amenities are offered with that compact precision that only living on a boat can inspire. Both staterooms, fore and aft, have a queen bed. Aft has its own bathroom, fore uses the bathroom in the main cabin. When the weather's good, enjoy the huge breakfast on deck and watch the boaters head to sea. *On the K dock, PO Box 1212, Friday Harbor, WA 98250; 360/378-5661; www.slowseason.com; $$; AE, MC, V; checks OK.*

ORCAS ISLAND

Named not for the whales (the large cetaceans tend to congregate on the west side of San Juan Island and are rarely spotted here) but for a Spanish explorer, Orcas has a reputation as the most beautiful of the four big San Juan Islands. It's also the largest (geographically), boasting 58 square miles, and the hilliest, with 2,407-foot Mount Constitution as the centerpiece of Moran State Park. Oddly, the island has little public beach. But the forested state park is huge, thanks to a gift early in this century from shipping tycoon Robert Moran.

Shaped like a pair of inflated lungs, with the cute little village of Eastsound running up the breastbone, Orcas has its ferry landing where it's most convenient for boats to pull in, 8 miles from town. Most people bring their cars to the island, especially if they want to head up the big hill outside of Eastsound for Moran State Park, but you can walk on the ferry and rent a bicycle above the landing; the traffic on the fairly level road to town ebbs and flows with the ferry's scheduled arrivals and departures. Walk-ons can also stay at the historic Orcas Hotel at the landing, with its restaurant, bar, and bakery, an easy stopover.

ACTIVITIES

Biking. You can rent bikes at the Orcas ferry landing from Dolphin Bay Bicycles, 360/376-4157, or in Eastsound from Wild Life Cycles, 360/376-4708. A good bike route that avoids traffic from the ferry terminal: the back road to Eastsound (via Dolphin Bay Road). Turn right off the ferry on the Horseshoe Highway to Killebrew Lake (about 2½ miles) and turn left on Dolphin Bay Road, which travels past fields, old orchards, several ponds, and woodlots for about 5 miles. The road cuts back to the Horseshoe Highway to the village of Eastsound, where bikers must use extreme caution—especially during the ferry rush.

For a day trip, take your bikes to Shaw Island, where there's no traffic (and no eats or sleeps). Bikes and peds are free on inter-island crossings (and this one's only 10 minutes). Buy picnic items at the little grocery store on Shaw's dock, but be sure to bring your own water. Bike all day, then return to Orcas for dinner and to sack out.

The islands have been discovered— overrun in the summer, though nearly abandoned in the winter—prompting one Orcas Islander to refer to her home as "Orcapulco" in summer, "Orcatraz" in winter. For that reason, we recommend fall and spring as the best bet for visitors.

Jim Rorabaugh is a gifted wood-carver whose life-size (and larger) carvings of birds and fish are exquisite. Some are accurate right down to the last feather and scale; others are more playful. He carves at home on Crescent Beach. Stop by, but call first if you want to make sure he's home: 360/376-2464.

All 30 miles of hiking trails in Moran State Park, including those around Cascade Lake (2½ miles) and Mountain Lake (3½ miles), are open to mountain bikers during the winter months only (winter around here means Labor Day through Memorial Day). The pedal to the park from Eastsound, up Flaherty's Hill on the Horseshoe Highway (no shoulders), is a killer.

Arts and Crafts. Leo Lambiel was born in Los Angeles and is a former resident of New York City, the Isle of Rhodes in Greece, and, for the last 35 years, Orcas Island. A collector of fine wines and antique and contemporary Oriental rugs, he's also a champion of San Juan County artwork. More than 111 local artists are represented in his collection, which includes a 370-square-foot mural and a mosaic made with 1,900 pieces of glass. Visitors, personally guided by Mr. Lambiel, may see the collection, including sculpture installed on six levels of waterfront deck, a Greek temple, and a grotto. Plan one hour to look, two hours if you want to talk about art. $5 per person, by appointment only; 360/376-4544.

Bud McBride and Richard Schneider's Crow Valley Pottery has been in the same spot since 1958. They dig island clay to make their pots. The gallery's a kick—it's in the island's oldest log cabin, still on the spot where it was built 130 years ago. Jeffri Coleman and Michael Rivkin run the gallery, which has expanded from the cabin into the old farm shed and houses artwork (including garden art) from 70 artists from all over the world, but primarily the Puget Sound area—especially the work of glass artists. The third weekend in July is the highly zany goblet show, with wine from Lopez Island Vineyards filling the glasses, an on-site glass blower, and the Olga Symphony performing in the garden. Open every day during the summer. On the Horseshoe Highway to Eastsound from Orcas, just before the golf course—watch for signs; 360/376-4260.

The old house and outbuildings in the cedar grove at the end of West Beach Road are actually Trudy Erwin's pottery studio, called The Right Place, 360/376-4023. Look for whimsical pots, as well as Trudy's paper cutouts. For $5 each, children and adults can take a turn at the wheel here, too (summers only). Pots are dried overnight; you come back and glaze them the next day. Or wait for a quick raku firing. It's an island tradition since the

1950s. In the adjoining Naked Lamb, shopkeeper Sharon Douglas sells her own hand-spun wool from island sheep, as well as a huge selection of yarns, plus sweaters, vests, hats, socks, and other clothing made by skilled island knitters and weavers; 360/376-4606.

Also off West Beach Road is Orcas Island Pottery, 360/376-2813, where you'll see a fountain of teapots and pitchers that pour water into cups, and walk on paving stones imbedded with colorful shards. You might even find the polka-dot and plaid work of Joe and Marclay Sherman, Orcas potters from the 1930s, on display. The log cabin on the place was built in the 1860s and traded from the Arnys' farm for a set of dishes. Julia Crandall bought the place in 1953; today her granddaughter Syd Exton shares the place with other potters. Sit in the swing and church pews overlooking the water and take in the view. Seconds are for sale in an old boat. Take Enchanted Forest Road to West Beach Road and watch for signs.

Mike Boyd has sold his handmade tile at Orcas Island Artworks, 360/376-4408, in the old strawberry baling shed at Olga, for as long as we can remember. Other longtime Orcas artists selling their work here are Kathy Schradle (canvas bags), Jerry Weatherman (pots), Leslie Little (ceramics), and Bill Glass (glass). Go through Moran State Park on Doe Bay Road to find Olga.

Bird-watching. Wood ducks, mergansers, and warblers nest in the woods around Killebrew Lake (less than 3 miles to the east of the ferry landing). Pick up something to eat at the grocery store or bakery at the landing, rent a bike, and have a very pleasant morning.

Watch for great horned owls, pileated woodpeckers, flickers, and thrushes in the coniferous forest around Cascade and Mountain Lakes in Moran State Park.

Dense rafts of wintering seabirds and grebes, cormorants, and loons spend the off-season in Deer Harbor and West Sound. Uncommon birds have been spotted in the oak and juniper trees along the shoreline. While you're in Deer Harbor, ask directions to the Frank Richardson Wildfowl Sanctuary, the largest freshwater marsh and most productive breeding grounds in the San Juans. The marsh is a thrilling place to be when the red-winged blackbirds, nesting in cattails, sing their throaty songs.

Marinas. Orcas Island's West Sound Marina, 360/376-2314, and Rosario Resort & Spa, 800/562-8820, both offer

Oyster farmers pick up their crop with wheelbarrows at low tide. You watch from the tiers of rock on Madrona Point, which divides East Sound into Ship Bay and Fish Bay (the bay in front of the village of Eastsound). Look for seabirds, seals, and otters.

transient moorage with power and water, groceries, showers, marine supplies, and fuel. Rosario charges a $17 landing fee, but hey, that buys you five passes to use the hotel's three swimming pools and spa. Deer Harbor's facilities, 360/376-4110, are a little more extensive, with a broader selection of supplies. There is also limited moorage and the opportunity to resupply and refuel at the dock next to the ferry landing.

Fresh Seafood. Fishermen sell fresh crab, clams, and mussels from pickup trucks parked in Eastsound (and at Island Market). Charlene and Bill Bawden sell oysters from a little cabin on Crescent Beach (between Eastsound and the road to Moran State Park). Grill them or make an oyster stew by lightly sautéing shucked oysters in butter, adding milk to cover, and heating gently; season with salt and pepper.

The county's Otter Crossing warning sign on Crescent Beach has been stolen so many times, they've changed it to Wildlife Crossing, a less desirable steal.

Music. Well-known musicians, such as Lionel Hampton and Ranch Romance, have performed at the 230-seat Orcas Center on Mount Baker Road in Eastsound, between gigs in Vancouver, BC, and Seattle. The acoustics are fine, and the audiences enthusiastic. Orcas has good local music—and plays—as well, with both amateur and professional talent. Islanders watch the old gas tank at the junction of Terrill Beach Road and the Horseshoe Highway for event information. You can just call 360/376-2281.

You've got to think ahead to get tickets to the Orcas Island Chamber Music Festival, held annually the first week in September. There's nothing quite like staying in a rustic cabin, say, at Beach Haven Resort, and trundling to Eastsound's Orcas Center to listen to Schubert, Bach, or Tchaikovsky strings at sunset. For tickets, call 360/376-2281. For information, call 360/376-6636.

Rosario Resort. The man responsible for Moran State Park was shipbuilding tycoon Robert Moran. His old mansion is now the centerpiece of Rosario Resort, just west of the park. Unfortunately, the resort hasn't lived up to its extravagant publicity or prices. Regardless, it's worth a sight-seeing trip to examine the Moran Museum or grab a bite to eat in the Moran Lounge or the Poolside Bar & Grill (in summer). And don't miss the free hour-long concerts nightly on the enormous pipe organ in the mansion, decked out in memorabilia and mahogany trim. Rosario Resort, 360/376-2222.

Spiritual Retreat. Dora Kunz, now 96, in 1927 found and helped purchase the 78 acres overlooking East Sound for the Theosophical Society's summer camp, called Indralaya. She and her brother, Harry Van Gelder, worked all over the world as healers; she still teaches healing workshops periodically at Indralaya. The Orcas Island Foundation's summer and fall lecture series also take place at the camp, and include five-day workshops on all sorts of things—from Tibetan Buddhism to creativity. Lodging is primitive, and the vegetarian food is direct from the camp's organic garden and old orchard. Lodgers help with the chores. (Route 1, Box 86, Eastsound, WA 98245; 360/376-4526.)

Local stores carry tapes of Orcas boat-dweller and composer Heather Stansbury's folk ballads and the Olga Symphony's folksy banjo, guitar, bass, and fiddle music.

Island Singer. Singer and composer Susan Osborn, whose Sony album *Wabi* won Japan's equivalent of the Grammy, performs for special occasions on the island, accompanying herself on the guitar. She's an impressive voice whose latest compositions reflect her Orcas Island interior life. Limited editions of her albums are available from Songhouse Productions, Inc., Orcas Island. Susan is the driving force behind The Living Room, a small performance hall in Eastsound. For information on recordings and events, call 360/376-5180.

Shopping. Blake Shore's got an eye for good stuff, all right. Her little shop, Rutabaga, 360/376-5737, has moved from Eastsound to a spread of historic buildings near Deer Harbor and "is a cross between Smith & Hawken and Williams-Sonoma with a whole lot of Blake," according to one islander. Look here for local biological field illustrations and wooden kayak models made by island artists, beeswax candles, oyster knives, and Egyptian cotton towels among beautiful things gleaned from gift shows and catalogs. Blake's playful sense of color makes this place special.

Darvill's Rare Print Shop (Horseshoe Highway, Eastsound, 360/376-2351) originated in San Francisco in 1925 and moved to the island in 1942. Some music parchments in the shop are from the 16th century; floral prints date back to 1610. It's a fascinating place, where engravings range from $25 to $3,000. Ask owner Dale Pederson about any place—such as Ireland—and he'll pore

Rent your kid a rowboat or paddleboat, and swim at the sandy beach at Moran State Park's Cascade Lake (the gently sloping shoreline on the highway side near North End Campground is a great spot for young children). A little store sells hot dogs, pop, and other favorite snacks.

At minus tides, you can walk from the beach on a natural sand bridge out to Indian Island (originally called Yap Island because of the seals' constant yapping). Some people claim this beach is a particularly energized spot. See if your picnic digests better here. Hurry back before the tide returns.

through five or six files of prints from the vault, many of them from the 17th through 19th centuries. The adjoining Darvill's Book Store, 360/376-2135, is one of the best in the islands. Both are open year-round; hours vary with the season, but Darvill's is usually open when nothing else is.

Quick Snacks. Two old storefronts on Orcas Island's waterfront—located originally to accommodate those coming by boat from other parts of the island—have been cleared of their groceries and turned into cafe/deli/espresso shops. Stop at West Sound Store & Cafe for breakfast fixings, seared fish tacos for lunch (heaped with fresh fish as good or better than in Mexico), and the best pie in the islands. There's a wide deck here overlooking the bay and nice rooms for rent upstairs. The proprietors are the former owners of Bainbridge Island's famed Streamliner Diner. The counter at the nearby Olga Store's glassed-in porch overlooks the water too.

Picnic. On the hill between the ferry holding area and the landing are picnic tables in a grove of madrona trees. There are three nice places to picnic in Eastsound: the grassy field surrounding the island's history museum has picnic tables; if you want to eat on the waterfront, there's a small city park just as you enter Eastsound (the town), facing East Sound (the water), with access to bleached white driftwood tossed up on the beach (about the only little stretch of public beach on the entire island); and there's Madrona Point. The Lummi Tribe saved Madrona Point from condo development in 1988 when they paid $6 million for their ancient burial site to preserve it in a forever-wild state. The road narrows to a path that extends to the tip of the rocky promontory. It's a gorgeous spot, with a grove of red-barked madronas leaning over three little pocket beaches filled with driftwood. To find it, follow Prune Alley across the Horseshoe Highway at Eastsound. You'll know you're on the right road when you see the white Odd Fellows Lodge on the right. The paved road leads to a county dock. You'll see a sign marking the day park's boundary. Please use with care.

You'll also find picnic grounds at Cascade Lake in Moran State Park. You can find everything you need for a picnic at Eastsound's market, the grown-up version of dear old Templins, where the grocery aisles were so jammed you had to pull your cart behind you. The megamarket à la the mainland was nicknamed the Temple, but now the shock has worn off and it seems just another small market. Island Market is on Prune Alley—read labels and look for island-made salsa, wine, and Lopez Larry's mustards and barbecue and seafood sauces.

Hiking. The most popular trails in Moran State Park, 360/376-2326, are the easy loop trail (3½ miles) around Mountain Lake and the even easier loop (2½ miles) around Cascade Lake. The Cascade Loop includes a section of highway on the north lakeshore, but there's a trail up and along the hillside behind the campground if you want to stay off the road. The 2-plus-mile hike into Twin Lakes from the Mountain Lake boat ramp is a route less taken. Two trails also lead to the top of Mount Constitution, about a 6-mile walk uphill, but cheaters can join the trail from the road as close as ½ mile from the top (or find a ride to the top and walk down). Look for lady's slippers, white Indian pipe, and mushrooms near the trail around Mountain Lake in Moran State Park, as well as drifts of foxglove in sunlit areas. Spring and early summer are best. Pick up a trail guide from the park ranger's office at Cascade Lake; trails on the map are labeled "easy" and "steep." Believe them. If you want the layout of the land, buy a USGS Mount Constitution quadrangle map, available in Eastsound from Gulls & Buoys Gifts, 360/376-2199.

Sand Dollars. Go to Crescent Beach, just east of Eastsound (on the Horseshoe Highway), and rent one of their stable, wide, little plastic boats—especially great for beginners. The bay is an environmental nursery for all kinds of sea life, from Dungeness crab to herring. No dangerous tide rips, eddies, or whirlpools here. Skim over one of the largest sand dollar beds in the world, and paddle to nearby Madrona Point at low tide to see colonies of purple and orange sea stars clinging to the rocks.

Island History. In the 1950s, several log cabins were moved from all over the island to Eastsound to form the Orcas Island Historical Museum, one of the best local museums we've ever seen. One room is dedicated to island pioneers, one to early island resorts, another to Jim Geoghegan's photographs from the early 1900s (you can buy prints made from original glass plates and nitrate negatives). Orchardists once produced fruit

Follow North Beach Road in Eastsound north to the few square feet of public beach for views of Mount Baker and Sucia Island. (This beach is a prime example of why Washington State should have allowed all beaches to be public.) The entire island of Sucia is a state park—it's just that you need to have a boat and fight the riptide to get there.

here: look for the room of boxes, preserves, labels, and stencils—it's a beauty. A homesteader cabin and island store have been re-created here, too. On North Beach Road in Eastsound. Call for hours, 360/376-4849.

A teacher's chart in the Crow Valley School Museum, an 1888 schoolhouse, describes things every educated child should know: how to estimate the amount of lath needed to finish a room, the weight of coal, and how to cut rafters. The one-room school, restored by descendants of the pioneer Burt family, contains original desks, an organ, a blackboard (signed by some of the former students), and photographs of early classes (3 miles west of Eastsound on Crow Valley Road; 360/376-4260; open Thursday through Saturday, summer afternoons).

 Picnic. Dennis Reigel makes birdhouses, architecturally to scale, of island landmarks, available at Crow Valley Pottery, 360/376-4260. Six of the real structures are on the National Register of Historic Places: the 1885 Emmanuel Church, 1904 Orcas Hotel, 1888 Schoolhouse, 1906 Rosario mansion, 1889 Alderbrook Victorian, and 1908 Doe Bay post office. A brochure listing directions to these and other architectural landmarks is available from the Orcas Island Historical Museum (North Beach Road, Eastsound, 360/376-4849).

Sight-seeing. There's room for two in the cockpit of the shiny red biplane with bright yellow wings—a spare-no-expense restoration of a 1929 TravelAir. You sit in front in your leather helmet with goggles and headset, and pilot Rod Magner, sitting in the backseat, regales you with stories as he flies over the islands for 30 minutes, twisting and circling—but no loop-the-loops. It's a breathtaking half hour. In the last nine years, 7,000 people have flown with Magner, an ex-Navy jet pilot who's been flying planes since he was a kid. Be sure to linger in his hangar, which some people call a museum—it holds Magner's private collection of aviation memorabilia. March to October only. Call Magic Air Tours, 360/ 376-2733 or 900/376-1929.

The spectacular 360-degree view from the stone tower, built by the Civilian Conservation Corps in the 1930s, on top of 2,407-foot Mount Constitution is not to be missed (even when it's fogged in down below, it's a spectacular day up top). From here, you can see the Cascades, the Olympics, San Juan archipelago, and Vancouver Island. You can drive to the top, but the paved road (6 miles) is closed from late fall to early spring (it gets slick and dangerous). You can hike to the top anytime via the steep 6-mile trail from Mountain Lake.

Camping. A warning: Most beachfront on Orcas is privately owned. A better bet for camping is inland at Moran State Park, with a few campsites at private resorts or on nearby small islands.

The lighthouse on Patos Island, 5 miles north of Orcas, is a West Coast classic, built in 1908. You'll need a boat, but it's well worth the trip.

Moran State Park's 136 campsites fill up fast in the summer, and for good reason. Nestled around Cascade and Mountain Lakes in deep forest, the camps are a small part of the 4,800-acre park, which includes nearly 30 miles of hiking trails, including two trails to the top of Mount Constitution. The woodland camp feels like something out of the 1930s, and indeed it is, with bathhouse and three updated rest rooms with cheap hot showers. We wish campsites were farther apart (as at every campground, you get neighbors with pink plastic tricycles, battery-operated fluorescent lights, radios, and dogs), but at least here you're side by side among big firs and cedars, and the lakes are clear and cold. Open fires are allowed in fire pits, subject to statewide bans during dry spells. Bring your own firewood or buy kindling and split logs from the park concessionaire; no scavenging fallen limbs for your fire.

A small, primitive campground at Obstruction Pass Marine State Park can be reached by boat or by a ¾-mile hike. There are pit toilets for nine campsites, but no fresh water. The 80-acre park, managed by the Department of Natural Resources, has the best saltwater beach (with great tide pools) available to the public on Orcas Island. No reservations, and no fees.

Fishing. Fish for trout year-round in Mountain Lake and Twin Lakes (a 2½-mile hike), summers only in Cascade Lake. Campsites are available year-round (but you must write at least two weeks ahead in the summer for reservations: Moran, Star Route Box 22, Eastsound, WA 98245, no phone reservations). Call 360/376-2326 and leave your name and address on the answering machine to request a complete packet of information, which will be mailed to you.

ISLAND KAYAKING

Before 1900, hearty islanders rowed between islands and the mainland. Today one of the most satisfying (and low-impact) ways to explore the San Juan Islands is by sea kayak. Outfitters abound (check the phone book), but we caution you to choose your guides carefully—experienced kayakers are wary of treacherous tidal currents, whirlpools, and sudden tempests, and we've heard reports of guides unfamiliar with the waters taking life-threatening chances. Make sure yours offers a complete safety lesson before the trip, including self-rescue. Trips range from beginners' 3-hour trips to overnight camp trips. We recommend two companies because of their sterling safety records and outstanding marine biology narration: Shearwater Sea Kayak Tours (14 years in the islands), Eastsound, Orcas Island, 360/376-4699; and Sea Quest Expeditions, Friday Harbor, San Juan Island, 360/378-5767.

Camping Resorts. West Beach Resort, 360/376-2240, on the west side of the island overlooking President Channel, has about 22 camping sites with water and electricity and 30 tent sites, some in the woods, in a friendly, family atmosphere. Reservations are strongly advised. Doe Bay Village Resort & Retreat, 360/376-2291, on the island's east side, has 6 campsites with fire pits on each bluff overlooking the little bay, and open camping in two grassy fields—just throw down your tent and claim your turf—great for kayakers and other drop-ins: first-come, first-get. Rest-room facilities are nearby, with clothing-optional sauna and hot tub.

Doe Bay. The location of Doe Bay, an age-old hippie resort, is great, with plenty of trails, two small beaches, a campground, a small store, a good vegetarian restaurant, and an outdoor mineral-spring hot tub (bathing suits optional). However, the minimalist cabins are a bit rickety, have no screens, and are not exactly sanitary. We suggest you stay elsewhere but enjoy the use of the hot tub during a slow winter week (small extra fee); 360/376-2291.

Marine Parks. You can scoot over to the 1-acre Freeman Island Marine State Park, 300 yards off Orcas's northwest shore; or Jones Island Marine State Park, ½ mile off the southwest tip of Orcas. The park on Patos Island to the north has trails and 4 campsites (but no water). Most of Matia Island's 150 acres are wildlife refuge, but the island does have two buoys, 10 campsites, and fresh water. All of these islands are accessible only by private boat. Look for these islands on nautical charts available at Gulls & Buoys Gifts (Horseshoe Highway, Eastsound, 360/376-2199).

Fishing. Calvin McLachlan lives at Deer Harbor on land his great-grandfather homesteaded in 1888. In the days before he had an outboard motor and fishing pole, he used to tie a pink-and-white lucky Louie plug on a heavy cord with a couple of ounces of lead, and hang it over the side of his rowboat at daybreak. The fish were so plentiful, he says, he could catch four or five 10-pound silver salmon before breakfast, sometimes a 30-pound king. Today salmon need help to survive, and Jim Youngren's privately owned salmon hatchery near Crescent Beach releases about four million smolt annually. They're finger-size salmon that should return to Orcas Island in two to six years. Cal says overfishing has severely damaged the runs—the salmon don't have a chance against sophisticated electronic equipment. For those still willing to fish with a pole, he recommends Thatcher Pass (between Decatur and Blakely Islands), Lopez Pass (between Lopez and Decatur Islands), off Cattle Point, and Lime Kiln on San Juan Island, and all around Stuart and Waldron Islands west of Orcas. Of course, you need a boat unless ocean temperatures drive the herring, salmon's favorite lunch, into the bays—that's when fishers can catch blackmouth right off the dock.

Best Golf Course in the Islands. San Juan Island and Lopez both have fairly flat golf courses, but the best in the islands is the alternate tee, nine-hole Orcas Island Golf Club, built on 53 acres of a valley homestead. Owner Robert Blake (his dad built the course after family and friends spent months picking rocks) says the best stroke hole is number two, with an elevated drive, pond, and lake hazards. Pros love it. People play through the winter; summers require you to sign up for a teetime, although the course is relaxed and less crowded than mainland courses. Summers, Blake's wife, Doreen, serves beer and barbecued burgers and chicken from the clubhouse, the original 100-year-old farmhouse. On the Horseshoe Highway between Orcas and Eastsound; 360/376-4400.

Wildflowers. Because most of Orcas Island is either deeply wooded or grazed pasture, the best wildflower meadows are along Deer Harbor Road. In early spring look for bright yellow skunk cabbage in the swampy spots and fields of buttercups. Blackberries, with their star-shaped white blossoms tinted with lavender, and salmonberries, with hot pink blossoms, flower at the same time. Hedgerows of wild roses and snowberry line roads and fields. Drier hillsides are bright orange with California poppies. Please don't pick 'em.

Island Weddings. Weddings are no longer allowed on island ferries, but tying the knot on Orcas can be wonderfully romantic. It's all here—catering, cakes, flowers, and romantic venues. Marry at the Victorian Valley Chapel, 360/376-5157, on private property a few miles from the ferry landing, or the gardens at Green Dolphin Farm, 360/376-4904. Or in picturesque community centers like the one on West Sound, which doubles as the yacht club. For gorgeous wedding bouquets, islanders recommend Vicki Clancy's Blossom and Branches, 360/376-5075 (she also keeps lists of where you can get married on the island).

Farm and Garden. Stacey Coleman and Shelley Kimball, former Seattle restaurant owners, figured out what they really wanted to do—bail out of Seattle and combine their interests into a teahouse and pond-plant nursery exhibiting specimen plants such *Gunnera manicotta*—a South American giant that looks like rhubarb on steroids. Their property, near Olga, is an old farmstead with three ponds and a creek running through it—all planted and landscaped with wild grasses, water lilies, and several dozen varieties of iris. The old barn is filled with Asian pots, bamboo waterspouts, and other pondelicious things; visitors can wander the grounds, then have a spot of tea served in vintage china cups, with cookies under porch umbrellas on the back deck of the farmhouse. There are places to sit in the garden with your picnic (you bring it) and your bride: you can reserve the garden for weddings. Open seven days a week summers, call for winter hours (3607 Point Lawrence Road, 360/376-2342).

Freshly cut flowers and unusual plants grown at Rocky Top Gardens are sold in a kiosk on Doe Bay Road (across from Orcas Island Artworks). The nursery is open by appointment only, 360/376-2042, offering such things as double-petaled salmonberry and other native cultivars.

RESTAURANTS

BILBO'S FESTIVO ☆

Orcas Islanders and visitors who have been coming here for the last 25 years speak of this cozy little place with reverence. Its decor and setting—mud walls, Mexican tiles, arched windows, big fireplace, handmade wooden benches, and spinning fans in a small house with a flowered courtyard—are charming, and the Navajo and Chimayo weavings on the walls are indeed from New Mexico. The fare includes a combination of Mexican and New Mexican influences, with improvisation on enchiladas, burritos, *chiles rellenos*, and mesquite-grilled specials. In summer, lunch is served *taqueria*-style, grilled to order outdoors, then heaped with the condiments of your choice. *North Beach Rd and A St, PO Box 511, Eastsound, WA 98245; 360/376-4728; $; full bar; MC, V; local checks only; lunch, dinner every day (dinner only off-season).*

CAFE OLGA ☆

You're likely to experience a wait at Cafe Olga, a popular midday stop for locals and visitors alike. Luckily, this country kitchen is part of the Orcas Island Artworks, a sprawling cooperative crafts gallery in a picturesque renovated strawberry-packing barn, so you can browse while you work up an appetite. The wholesome international home-style entrées range from a rich Sicilian artichoke pie to a chicken enchilada with black bean sauce to a Greek salad. For dessert, try a massive piece of terrific blackberry pie. *East of Moran State Park at Olga Junction, Olga, WA 98279; 360/376-5098; $; beer and wine; MC, V; local checks only; lunch every day (closed Jan–Feb).*

Every hip town lays claim to a steamy, hip bakery, and Eastsound has Roses Bakery Café, 360/376-4220. Locals prefer the outdoor patio for blueberry scones, fresh baguettes, and enormous bowls of latte.

CHRISTINA'S

 Built above a 1930s gas station in Eastsound, Christina's offers the bewitching blend of provincial locale and urban sophistication that marks the finest rural destinations. The view of the bay and craggy islet from the dining room and deck is sublime; more often than not, Christina Orchid's classic continental food is, too. Singing scallops, gathered off Guemes Island, might be gently steamed in their elegant shells with fragrant hints of thyme and garlic; king salmon might arrive adorned with tender coils of fiddlehead fern. A recent fillet of beef in Gorgonzola cream was a masterpiece of flavor and texture, the kind of dish that has made Christina's reputation as the finest dining room in the islands. You will be dropping an easy $100 (for two) to eat here. Servings tend toward the generous, with a nice selection of appetizers sized right to split or enjoy as your own light meal. *310 Main St (North Beach Rd and Main St), Eastsound, WA 98245; 360/376-4904; www.christinas.net; $$$; full bar; AE, DC, MC, V; checks OK; dinner every day (Thurs–Mon in winter).*

SHIP BAY OYSTER HOUSE

Ship Bay has developed a reputation as a great spot for fresh fish and local oysters. Lovers of the briny mollusks will be in oyster heaven: baked, stewed, pan-fried, or au naturel (try an oyster shooter, served up in a shot glass with Clamato and sake), there's an oyster for every palate. The Pacific Coast locale (a comfortable remodeled farmhouse on 8 acres of orchards overlooking Ship Bay) belies the Atlantic Coast ambience. The clam chowder—a New Englandy version—included with every entrée—might be the best in the West, and the kitchen obviously never learned about portion control (just order a small slab of spicy-hot barbecue baby back ribs with its exceptional accompaniment of black beans and salsa, and you'll get our drift). Locals swear the best deal on the island is appetizer fare in the lounge or outdoor seating on the patio. You can hardly miss here. The year 2000 brought 14 deluxe rooms (one an executive suite) with king beds, fireplaces, and whirlpool baths. *326 Olga Road (just east of Eastsound on Horseshoe Hwy), Eastsound,*

WA 98245; 360/376-5886; $$; full bar; AE, MC, V; checks OK; dinner every day.

LODGINGS

BEACH HAVEN RESORT ☆

Regardless of the time of year, this funky family retreat with its long pebble beach, canoes and rowboats, and lack of maid service reminds us of summer camp: no TV, no telephones, no fussy amenities. A designated family section sports a wonderful playground. Expect a seven-day minimum stay in summer, and consider coming in the off-season (two-night minimum), when rates prove especially affordable (and you'll likely encounter fewer "campers"). Accommodations range from various grades of rustic—the woodstove-heated cabins, shielded by old-growth forest, are of the genuine log variety—to modern apartments, a "Spectacular Beachcomber" four-bedroom house, and a "Honeymoon Cabin," set back in the woods with a private path to its own private beach. The Honeymoon Cabin has a fully furnished kitchen, woodstove, Jacuzzi tub, and heated bathroom floor. *684 Beach Haven Rd (about 10 miles NW of ferry, at President Channel off Enchanted Forest Rd), Eastsound, WA 98245; 360/376-2288; relax@beach-haven.com; www.beach-haven.com; $$; MC, V; checks OK.*

CASCADE HARBOR INN ☆☆

Now this is the way to stay at Rosario, particularly if you have kids in tow. Forty-eight modern units—some studios with Murphy beds, some two-queen rooms, some in between—all have decks and water views, and many configure into multi-unit suites with fully equipped kitchens. Once managed by the sprawling Rosario Resort next door, this inn now shares only its vistas of pristine Cascade Bay and its beach access. Continental breakfast is included. *1800 Rosario Rd (just east of Rosario Resort along shore of Cascade Bay), Eastsound, WA 98245; 800/201-2120 or 360/376-6350; cascade@rockisland.com; www.cascadeharborinn.com; $$$; DIS, MC, V; checks OK.*

Stay on a working farm at Coffelt's Farm B&B (Route 1, Box 32, Crow Valley Road, 360/376-4357), owned by descendants of an Orcas Island pioneer family. Sydney and Vern raise sheep, hay, and chickens, and have an assortment of cats and dogs on their 197 acres. Be awakened by a rooster, and chow down on real farm food for breakfast.

CHESTNUT HILL INN BED & BREAKFAST ☆☆☆

Every romantic stereotype of B&B elegance is fulfilled in this renovated farmhouse, perched atop a pastoral rise not far from the ferry landing. Marilyn Loewke (islanders call her "Ms. Romance") and her husband, Dan, have fitted their five guest rooms with luxurious appointments large and small: feather beds, fireplaces, Egyptian-cotton linens, robes, slippers, liqueurs, loofahs. The fanciest, the Chestnut Suite, boasts a TV/VCR and stereo, chilled bottled water and champagne, and two-person Jacuzzi tub with a dimmer switch for the crystal chandelier above. Suffice it to say, folks either love the romantic overkill or loathe it. But even hardened chinz-haters appreciate the attention and good taste that have gone into every facet of this inn. Each of the rooms has been individually conceived and appointed. We favor the Chapel Room, with its double shower and view of the charming steepled chapel in the pear orchard. There's also a pond (complete with rowboat), a stable (complete with horses), and a gazebo (complete with a full schedule of elopements). Larger weddings are held in the chapel, which holds up to 65 people. Marilyn is a gifted cook: in addition to lavish breakfasts, she prepares dinners for guests in the off-season (November to April) as good as anything else on the island. *414 John Jones Rd (just over a mile east of ferry landing off Laport Rd), PO Box 399, Orcas, WA 98280; 360/376-5157; chestnut@pacificrim.net; www.chestnuthillinn.com; $$$; DIS, MC, V; checks OK.*

DEER HARBOR INN AND RESTAURANT ☆☆

Over the last five years Pam and Craig Carpenter have shored up this old rustic lodge, originally constructed in 1915 in an orchard of apple trees overlooking Deer Harbor. Lodge rooms are small, with peeled log furniture, but new cabins on the property have a nice beachy feeling—knotty pine walls, log furniture, wood stoves or fireplaces, and private hot tubs on the deck. The new two bedroom, two bathroom cabin, built right on the bluff, could be your second home—it's so roomy—with a fully-equipped kitchen, fireplace and deck (at a whopping $269 a night during high season; lodge rooms are about $100). All beds are heaped with comforters and quilts. Whether you stay in the cabins or lodge, breakfast is delivered to your door in a picnic basket with freshly baked goods and plenty of hot coffee, sparing you from face to face morning encounters with other guests. Dinners are served nightly in the old lodge's rustic dining room with a large view deck. Craig serves up generous portions of fresh seafood along with a variety of meat dishes; all are served with salad and homemade bread. Wine and beer lists are thoughtfully conceived. *From ferry landing, follow signs to Deer Harbor; 877/377-4110 or 360/376-4110; www.deerharborlodge.com; $$; beer and wine; AE, MC, V; checks OK; dinner every day (closed Jan, and variable off-season).*

NORTH BEACH INN ☆

[View] If you like funky, private settings with history and personality, North Beach Inn is the spot. Originally an apple orchard, then converted into a resort in the early '30s, North Beach Inn has remained relatively unchanged ever since. Eleven worn cabins are laid out on a prime stretch of the Gibson family beach. The spiffiest: Columbia, Frazier, and Shamrock (which has a loft that kids adore). Each cabin comes complete with a full kitchen, grill, Adirondack chairs on the beach (bonfires allowed), and a tremendous view. Also likely: duck-print flannel sheets, flimsy floral curtains, artwork and furniture probably picked up at a local garage sale. Bring Fido if you like. One-week minimum stay July and August, two-day minimum the rest of the year (closed after Thanksgiving through mid-February). *650 Gibson Rd (about a mile west of airport at North Beach Rd), PO Box 80, Eastsound, WA 98245; 360/376-2660; $$; no credit cards; checks OK.*

ORCAS HOTEL

It's a pretty 1904 Victorian originally built as a boarding-house, just above the ferry terminal, with period pieces inside and white wicker on the deck overlooking the water. Best of the dozen accommodations are the two new, larger rooms, which have private balconies and whirlpool tubs. We've received complaints about the cleanliness of the place, gardens aren't as well kept as they once were, and,

The old tank lying on its side at the junction of Terrill Beach Road and the Horseshoe Highway is a signboard for local events, from "Welcome home, Debbi" to the dates for local theater performances. Sometimes it's painted, sometimes banners are wrapped around it. Watch for announcements of brown-bag summer concerts on the lawn of Eastsound's historic Emmanuel Church on the waterfront.

well, the inn is looking a bit worn out, but new owners Doug and Laura Tidwell are still playing catch-up with needed upkeep. It's a small, romantic hotel with a continental breakfast in the adjoining cafe included in the summer rate (off-season, you're on your own)—and it's the only accommodation on Orcas Island within walking distance of the big boat. The cafe with its grandstand deck is the place to wait out the ferry with a beer or a sandwich. *PO Box 155 (Orcas ferry landing), Orcas, WA 98280; 360/376-4300; orcas@orcashotel.com; www.orcashotel.com; beer and wine; $$; AE, MC, V; checks OK.*

OUTLOOK INN ☆

If you want to stay in the Manhattan of Orcas—that's Eastsound, with its variety of walking-distance restaurants—you'll want to stay at the legendary Outlook Inn. The name, by the way, reflects the interests of Lewis Gittner and Starr Farish, psychics to the stars who purchased the circa 1888 property more than 30 years ago. Lewis has since moved on to Thailand and, like the proverbial hippies who once flocked to stay here, the inn has traded in its countercultural spirit for the luxuries money can buy. Though the old part of the inn with shared bathrooms is still available—and affordable—newer swanky suites have bang-up views, fireplaces, decks, whirlpool baths, and heated towel racks, and they command prices a hippie would surely protest. Perhaps because we remember its humble past, the renovated Outlook Inn feels a little soulless to us. The bar and restaurant have, as always, a loyal local clientele—a good sign, we think. *PO Box 210 (on Main St), Eastsound, WA 98245; 888/688-5665 or 360/376-2200; info@outlook-inn.com; www.outlook-inn.com; $$–$$$; DIS, AE, MC, V; local checks only.*

PALMER'S CHART HOUSE

A room with a private bath and a view of Deer Harbor, plus breakfast for two, for $80 per night, double; $60, single. On Orcas Island? In summer? Don and Majean Palmer's simple daylight basement guest rooms fit the bill. Two rooms, each with a private entrance, a private bath, and a full breakfast. The globe-trotting hosts, residents of Orcas for 24 years, enjoy swapping travel tales with guests. Don offers day sails on his 33-foot sloop, the *Amante*, at $35 per person. *102 Upper Rd, PO Box 51, Deer Harbor, WA 98243; 360/376-4231; $; no credit cards, checks OK.*

SPRING BAY INN ☆☆☆

 It's a long dirt road getting here, but rarely is a drive so amply rewarded. Situated where 57 wooded acres meet the sea is the handsome Spring Bay Inn, as stylishly appointed indoors as it is scenic outside. The interior reflects the naturalist sensibilities of innkeepers Sandy Playa and Carl Burger, an engaging and youthful pair of retired state park rangers whose crunchy-granola lifestyle sets them apart from other upscale B&B owners. The angular great room, with its fieldstone fireplace and vaulted ceiling, showcases a stunning view of Spring Bay. Upstairs are four thoughtfully decorated guest rooms, each with its own bath and Rumford fireplace; two have private balconies. Downstairs is the Ranger's Suite, with 27 windows and its own hot tub. Come morning, coffee, muffins, and fresh fruit are delivered to each door—a little sustenance for the two-hour guided kayak tour around Obstruction Island, included with the room rate. (Beginners are welcome, kayaks and equipment provided, harbor seal and eagle sightings free of charge.) Return to the lodge for a big, healthy brunch. The property is adjacent to Obstruction Pass State Park, and is laced with hiking trails and teeming with wildlife. (Did we mention this is the place to come for a straight shot of fabled Northwest outdoorsiness?) After dark, ease tired muscles with a private soak under the stars in the bayside hot tub. *464 Spring Bay Trail (follow Obstruction Pass Rd to Trailhead Rd, take right fork onto Spring Bay Trail), PO Box 97, Olga, WA 98279; 360/376-5531; $$$; AE, DIS, MC, V; checks OK.*

TURTLEBACK FARM INN ☆☆

Located inland amid tall trees, rolling pastures, and ponds, Turtleback offers seven spotless rooms dressed in simple sophistication and stunning antiques. It also offers efficiency: Turtleback's veteran innkeepers, Bill and Susan Fletcher, have thought of everything, from cocoa, coffee, and fresh fruit for nibbling to flashlights for evening forays. Their curt personal style may leave them wanting in bed (and breakfast)side manner, but it didn't cramp us too much on a recent visit. What did cramp us was our room, the aptly named Nook. It really is worth the extra $50 or more to go up a notch or two: choose either one of the larger upstairs rooms or one of two downstairs rooms with private decks overlooking the meadow and the lambs a-prancing. Susan cooks magnificent breakfasts, and serves them on the deck in sunny weather. Members of the Turtleback Fan Club, take note: a new four-suite building has been added to the farm in the orchard, several hundred feet from the main farmhouse, sided with natural cedar that will weather like a barn. Inside are spacious rooms with fir flooring, trim, and doors, and each is furnished with a Vermont Casting stove, king bed, bar-size refrigerator, and spacious bath with large claw-foot tub and shower; all have private decks. Children are welcome in suites by prior arrangement to insure privacy and quiet for other guests. *1981 Crow Valley Rd (from the ferry terminal go left to Deer Harbor Rd, make a left, go left again on Crow Valley Rd, 6 miles from ferry terminal), Eastsound, WA 98245; 800/376-4914 or 360/376-4914; www. turtlebackinn.com; $$$; AE, DIS, MC, V; checks OK.*

WINDSONG BED & BREAKFAST ☆

A 1917 schoolhouse-turned-B&B (the first to be registered on Orcas), the Windsong has undergone another renovation and is now a warmly elegant bed-and-breakfast inn. Each of the four rooms is beautifully decorated and amply proportioned, with queen- or king-size beds; each has its own private bath and three have fireplaces. We favor the Rhapsody for its view through the trees to West Sound. A living room for guests offers a big TV and comfy couches; outside, a hot tub bubbles. Co-host Sam Haines is big on breakfast: he makes it in four courses. *213 Deer Harbor Rd (follow Deer Harbor Rd just west of Horseshoe Hwy), PO Box 32, Orcas Island, WA 98280; 800/669-3948 or 360/376-2500; reservations@windsonginn.com; www.windsonginn.com; $$; MC, V; checks OK.*

SHAW ISLAND

It's almost a religious experience when the ferry docks at Shaw Island. A formline-carved orca arches over the entrance, the deep-green water slaps gently against the rocks, and a Franciscan Sister of the Eucharist sometimes stands on the dock in her habit, waiting to pull the big metal lever that lowers the ramp. (Sometimes the nuns take a day off, and the ramp attendant is a young man in sneakers—but the orca and waves are still there.) With the exception of a county park and a wildlife refuge (closed to the public), the island is completely privately owned. No restaurants or lodgings, but a nice island to bike around.

ACTIVITIES

Shopping. Shaw's only shop is The Little Portion Store, operated by the Benedictine Sisters (the island supports two orders) and located at the ferry dock. In addition to very basic supplies, the store carries some surprisingly indulgent gourmet items, such as vinegars, mustards, hard cheeses, and herbs. These are produced by the nuns of Our Lady of the Rock, whose large farm is nearby.

Marina. Shaw Island's Little Portion Store, 360/468-2288, next to the ferry dock, has limited space for boats less than 24 feet, but no power or water (and gas in cans only). Open year-round.

Camping. It may be small, but it's a jewel. Located on the south end of the island, Shaw Island State Park offers day-park facilities, 12 campsites (first come, first get), and a stretch of sandy beach that is one of the best in the islands. The water is shallow for several hundred feet—warm enough for wading and swimming (if you have thick skin) in the summer, and heaven for toddlers. There are small-boat rentals, too.

LOPEZ ISLAND

Lopez Island, flat and shaped like a jigsaw-puzzle piece, is a sleepy, bucolic place. Bicyclists like Lopez for its gentle inclines and for the drivers who actually wave. The island is laced with country lanes and picturesque farms with weathered barns; on the west side is the island's sleepy Lopez Village, which in winter goes almost completely into hibernation. Changes loom, however. About the time Lopez's albino red-tailed hawk, a 26-year resident of the island, hit a fence and died in a raid on a chicken coop, a Microsoft founder began building his compound on Lopez. Techies have followed, with mega-houses popping up on the waterfront. Real estate prices soar and Lopez Village is creeping upscale—it has street names now and sidewalks. Singer Joni Mitchell (pave paradise, put up a parking lot) wrote the anthem of protest that artists, farmers, and other low-income folks on Lopez have adopted now. Still, there are more than 50 working farms on Lopez raising sheep and cattle and growing vegetables, herbs, and perennials. And it's a lovely place for a country bike ride.

The Lopez wave is meant for resident and visitor alike, a simple acknowledgment of your existence. Wave back, but not like a princess on a parade float. As a car approaches, keep your hand on the wheel and raise your fingers in greeting.

For pickups, deliveries, and car rentals, call Angie's Cab, 360/468-2227.

ACTIVITIES

Biking. Lopez has the easiest bicycling in the islands: a 30-mile circuit suitable for the whole family to ride in a day. If you've left your bike in your garage, rent one at Lopez Bicycle Works, 360/468-2847 (look for the yellow tricycle on top of their sign out front). Mountain bikes, tandems, and kids' bikes are available, as are repairs and sales. On Fisherman Bay Road next to the Lopez Islander Resort & Marina.

Camping and Beach Walking. Lopez has numerous but small public parks with beach access. Two new day parks (Otis Perkins and Upright Channel) are great for exploring, with good beach access. You can camp at Odlin County Park or Spencer Spit State Park on the north end of the island (see Island Camping, page 14). The wind blows right off the strait onto Agate Beach on the island's southwest tip, so the waves are bigger there than about anywhere on the island. It's a pleasant, rocky crescent with public access at the south end, and a great place to watch sunsets.

The island's only campground with showers is on private land (Lopez Farm Cottages, 360/468-3555) close to the ferry landing and across the road from Lopez Island Vineyards. Primitive campsites are in a grove of second-growth cedars overlooking a meadow where sheep graze, with cooking facilities (barbecues, a deep sink), covered picnic area, and private (!) rest rooms with showers (none of the state park campgrounds have showers) clustered in a central building. Best of all, you park your car in a hidden lot and walk into the campground, so there's no dust. Adults only.

Arts and Crafts. At Chimera, 360/468-3265, a Lopez artists cooperative, members take turns working, so there's always someone interesting to talk with. Also look for revolving displays of local paintings at the little post office, library, and senior center in Lopez Village. The Bay Cafe's decor changes with the whim of the owner and the cooks, but the collection of Fiestaware plates above the door and the rowboat stay the same.

Shopping. At Phyllis Potter's Islehaven, you can buy a book and feed a dog. Phyllis's two long-nosed dogs—Russian wolfhounds Cavalier and Pippa—greet customers year after year. Cavalier is often snoozing under the store's "dog section." Islanders often bring these canines their leftover and frozen steaks. Interesting books, too (Lopez Village, 360/468-2132).

The public library's two book sales (Friday after Thanksgiving and July 4) have some real steals—islanders are voracious readers and recycle their books; 360/468-2265. Every year a Chicago disc jockey donates boxes of books sent to him for review.

On the Sunday after Memorial Day weekend, the Lopez Island Historical Museum holds an old-fashioned country auction at the American Legion Hall on the south end of Fisherman Bay. Islanders donate tools, furniture, and antiques; proceeds benefit the museum, 360/468-2049.

Ice Cream. Indulge in old-fashioned ice-cream sodas, thick milkshakes, banana splits, and hot fudge sundaes at Lopez Island Pharmacy's new old-fashioned ice-cream parlor (Lopez Village, 360/468-2644). Lopez Island Creamery's ice cream is higher in butterfat than Ben & Jerry's, with flavors such as mango and lemon, and is sold at the Islandale gas station store (Mud Bay Road, 360/468-2315; the only store on the island's south end) and at the Lopez Village Market.

🔭 **Bird-watching.** Lopez is particularly blessed with the protected tide flats of Fisherman Bay and narrow Fisherman Spit, accessible from Bayshore Drive. Park at Otis Perkins Day Park. In the bay you'll find horned grebes, double-crested cormorants, ducks, plovers, yellowlegs, dowitchers, peeps, terns, gulls, and ospreys. Herons are abundant—we've seen them catching mice in the salt marsh, dipping them into the bay repeatedly before swallowing them in one gulp. Along the spit are brants, snow buntings, and Lapland longspurs; in the exposed salt water on the western side are numerous seabirds. A paved road runs down the middle of the spit, making walking and watching easy. A strand of beach is public—between private property markers only. For a real event, always keep one eye on the sky. Peregrine falcons strike their prey, such as ducks, from the air, knocking them asunder. Ospreys fold their wings and dive into the water to grab fish with their talons. Eagles catch live prey, such as rabbits and mice, but they also scavenge carrion off the beach, pecking the sand like chickens.

For years, a 300-plus herd of Shetland ponies could be seen grazing in various Lopez pastures. In 1994, it was reduced to 50 when the ponies' elderly owner, Theodore Ritchie, could no longer care for them all. Islanders and mainland pony clubs adopted the feisty little guys—but they had to catch them first. Not many are around anymore.

🗑 **Picnics.** Locals like to boast that the best fresh breads (such as hazelnut baguettes) and pastries in the Pacific Northwest are from Holly B's Bakery. Dare you disagree? Open summers and a few days a week in fall and spring (Lopez Plaza, Lopez Village, 360/468-2133).

Buy fixings for picnics at Lopez Village Market (for hot chicken baked in Lopez Larry's Barbecue Sauce, and San Juan Islands Seafood's smoked salmon), or go organic and vegan across the road at Blossom Natural Food Store. Frankly, we like to skip the picnic effort and eat on the deck at Vortex, the little kitchen counter in Blossom with great fruit smoothies, huge sandwiches, heaps of imaginative salad greens, and carbo-loaded cookies.

🌳🔭 **Water Watching.** Walk ¼ mile through the woods (watch out for roots threading the trail) to Shark Reef Park, where powerful tidal currents between Lopez and nearby San Juan Island create a swirling cauldron of whirlpools, eddies, and water as swift as any river. From the cliffs, watch seabirds pop back up to the water's surface, seals haul out on the rocky Goose Island across the channel, and boats' white sails strut across the horizon. Islander persistence saved this special point at the end of Shark Reef Road from development.

Farm and Garden. From Lopez Community Land Trust, 360/468-3723, you can pick up a brochure and map showing the locations of 55 Lopez Island farms. Map icons tell you whether to phone first or just show up and whether products are sold on-site. Included is Keith Sternberg's farm yielding steam-threshed wheat and organic whole wheat flour, Jenny Harris's Bellwether Perennials display gardens of drought- and deer-tolerant plants, and Ken Akopiantz's Horse-Drawn Produce—organic salad greens, specialty potatoes, and veggies. Also look on the map for Bob and Ginger Riggins's Marshfield Farm for handwoven blankets from farm-raised Coopworth sheep; Green Magic Herbs for medicinal tinctures, massage oils, rosebud necklaces, and garlic braids; and Danah Feldman's basil by the pound. Yum.

Sample fresh island produce (and crafts) at the farmers market in Lopez Village, 10am to 4pm Saturdays, summer only. Dip into Cathy Clemens's homemade fruit juices (Stonecrest Farms), rhubarb and ginger jam, lemon and lime curd, and concentrated home-distilled fruit juices made from island-grown berries and orchard fruit. Sniff the unusually scented bars from Seraphim Soaps. In the fall you can buy Akane, Jonagold, and Melrose apples from the espaliered orchards of Arbordoun. Call for directions and harvest dates, 360/468-2508.

Marinas. Lopez Island has two marinas—Islands Marine Center, 360/468-3377, and Lopez Islander Resort & Marina, 360/468-2233. Located side by side on Fisherman Bay, each offers fuel, showers, shore power, and marine supplies; the Islander also has a cafe, pool, and lodging. The bay looks wide but it is tricky to negotiate the narrow channel through mudflats, and high westerly winds make it less than perfect for winter moorage. Both marinas are about ½ mile from groceries and town. Open year-round.

ISLAND WINES

Wines labeled as being from Friday Harbor or Orcas Island are tourist gimmicks. The grapes are grown and the wine is made in the Yakima Valley. Lopez Island Vineyards, on the other hand, planted early ripening Madeleine Angevine and German Siegerrebe grapes in the mid '80s that are now bearing enough fruit to make wine on the premises. Try the medium-dry white apple-pear wine made with fruit grown in San Juan County, as well as raspberry, chardonnay, and a lusty cabernet and sauvignon-merlot as well, all organic. Blackberry dessert wine too. Vintner Brent Nilan learned his trade in Bordeaux, France, and the Napa Valley. Open for tasting. Gift shop features local art. Call for hours, 360/468-3644.

Island potter Nancy Bingham says that sometimes when she walks the beach in the dark, she can hear the whales' deep sighs when they surface offshore. Orcas tend to travel along the western shore of Lopez to the southern tip in pursuit of food.

Fishing. On Hummel Lake, kids like to toss their catch (or their parents') to an eagle that lives in the trees east of the lake; he'll fly down and scoop it up (but hopefully not off the end of your line). Fish year-round for bass or trout. Buy gear and fishing licenses at Islands Marine Center, Fisherman Bay Road, 360/468-3377.

Educational Vacations. Great boat. Good food. Great guy. That's islanders' consensus on Monte Hughes's educational vacation biz. Monte was born on Blakely Island to a homesteading family and lived on Lopez, and he knows the rum-running history of the islands like no one else. He used to do tours of the islands; now he does four-day kayak, painting, or photography workshops of the San Juan Islands aboard his 100-foot *Mystic Sea* cruiser. Best of all, guests stay overnight on the *Tahoma*, the old Anderson Island prison shuttle (a ferryboat) that's been converted into a floating B&B with eight staterooms, rest rooms with showers, and comfortable dining room. The *Tahoma* moves to a new location each day. $1,550 for four intense days, including food, lodging, and instruction. Call 360/466-3042 or 360/466-9104 for details.

Native Art. Three-day weekend seminars are held January to March on Northwest Native American art. They run the gamut from beginning to professional-level carving; rattle,

The only place on Lopez to get the Sunday New York Times *and the* Los Angeles Times *(and donated copies of* The Wall Street Journal) *is at the Lopez Island Library, 360/468-2265. This former schoolhouse is a cozy place to read. Nonresidents pay a refundable $10 fee to check out books while on the island.*

drum, and flute construction; basketry; and design. Workshops are taught by "top people who know their stuff, many of them Native American carvers," says Gregg Blomberg, who specializes in bowl carving and bentwood box making. Blomberg, a nonnative, is also a toolmaker. His straight and crooked knives and adzes are in the toolbox of every woodcarver of merit in the country. Kestral Tool, 180 Snowberry Lane, Lopez Island, WA 98261; 360/468-2103.

Goings On. Don't visit Lopez for its doings, but if you find yourself in need of entertainment, be sure to scrutinize the bulletin board outside the Lopez Village Market (Lopez Road at Fisherman Bay). Check it religiously or you'll miss most island events—from chamber music at Grace Church to Madrona Farm's bulb sales. Also check local newspapers for listings of events, workshops, and classes. Five acres were donated to the Lopez Community Center Association for the outdoor pavilion in the village (grass with a bandstand). New kids on the block have given generously to a performing arts center.

Shopping. The Lopez consumer motto is "Look for a shop till you drop." Whatever there is to buy is in Lopez Village, on Fisherman Bay. We expect this to change. They've added sidewalks; shops will follow. Best bets now: for goofy, fun, edgy goods visit Fish Bay Mercantile across the road from the museum. Islanders say the Thrift Shop in the Lopez Village water tower gets some great things from well-heeled summer people leaving it all behind—and all proceeds are donated to charity. Even better, drop stuff off there.

Island History. A whopping 34 sites are squeezed onto the Lopez Island Historical Museum's self-guided drive-by tour of historic landmarks. By 1930, Lopez had 134 farms and exported cream, eggs, poultry, veal, pork, pea seed, vetch, oats, barley, and wheat. A few farmhouses are on the tour, many of them in the island's south-center. Look for brochures at the museum in Lopez Village, 28 Washburn Place, 360/468-2049, or at the library. The first car in the San Juan Islands was a 1903 Orient Buckboard, an odd contraption that looks like a wagon with a tiller. You can see it, along with a foot-powered cow-milking machine, other farm tools, and a hands-on mechanical-gadget table, *inside* the historical museum (donations at the door; call for hours, 360/468-3447).

Also featured here is the albino red-tailed hawk that was sighted on the island for more than 26 years. A frequent visitor of a local chicken coop, the hawk miscalculated and crashed into a fence. Stuffed and under glass in the museum, the hawk is surrounded by local relics that include scale models of local fishing boats: gillnetters and salmon reef netters.

The three wooden water towers in Lopez Village are original, built between 1914 and 1916 by descendants of the Weeks family, who homesteaded the village site in 1850. The farmhouse is gone, but islanders are fond of the old towers. A T-shirt shop is in one, another houses the thrift store, and the third, adjacent to the grocery store, stands empty.

The island's only grocery store (Lopez Village Market, on Fisherman Bay) closes at 7pm, and restaurants are closed or have shortened hours in winter months. Reservations are essential during the summer.

RESTAURANTS

THE BAY CAFE ☆☆☆

Gossip central is Lopez Island Pharmacy's lunch counter.

 For years the twinkling Bay Cafe has been reason alone to come to this serene isle, and we hope that remains true under new owners and the new location. The cafe has moved down the row of shops to the beach end—not far, but the new modern digs are a far cry from the old. There's a spacious interior with the same rack of Fiestaware plates and rowboat suspended from the ceiling, and a great sunset view of the entrance to Fisherman Bay (diners in the past used to leave their food on their plates and go outside to catch the sunset). But the surprise of finding such extraordinary food in such an old rattletrap building was what delighted us most. The old place was intimate, too—diners sometimes passed forkfuls of dessert to other tables—and the new place seems less conducive to informality, although it's still a come-as-you-are kind of place—and people do. The chefs remain the same, though probably less harried in their spanking new kitchen that's 20 degrees cooler than the old one. Chefs do pledge to maintain their winning way with ethnic preparations from around the world. The menu, which changes every few months, might include pork and blue corn *posole*, grilled tofu with chickpea-potato cakes (vegetarians never suffer here), or a marvelous beef fillet draped in sweet caramelized onions and a roasted garlic–Roquefort sauce. Usually there are seafood tapas, which in a recent incarnation included basil-and-goat-cheese-stuffed prawns with saffron rice, and a delectable ricotta corn cake with smoked salmon and blackberry sauce. Prices are very reasonable, especially considering that dinners include both soup (perhaps a delicate chanterelle-spinach) and a fresh tossed salad. Most of the wait staff, some of them with the Bay Cafe for the last 14 years, have stayed on—though their patronage nearly tripled after the remodel. *90 Post Rd (junction of Lopez Rd S and Lopez Rd N, Lopez Village), Lopez Island, WA 98261; 360/468-3700; $$; spirits, beer, and wine; DIS, MC, V; checks OK; lunch, happy hour, dinner daily, summers; breakfast, lunch, dinner, Wed–Sun, winters (closed Jan).*

LODGINGS

BLUE FJORD CABINS ☆

Blue Fjord Cabins are the most secluded and tranquil getaway on Lopez. The two log cabins are tucked away up an unmarked dirt road, each concealed from the other by thick woods. They're of modern chalet design, clean and airy, with full kitchens. There's a three-night minimum stay in July and August. Doing nothing never had such a congenial setting. *862 Elliott Rd (Elliott Rd at Jasper Cove), Lopez Island, WA 98261; 888/633-0401 or 360/468-2749; www.interisland. net/bluefjord; $$; DIS; checks OK.*

EDENWILD INN ☆☆

 This majestic Victorian centerpiece of Lopez Village, surrounded with a lovely flower garden, features eight individually decorated rooms, some with fireplaces, all with private baths and beautifully stained hardwood floors. Though the inn is not on the water, the front rooms on the upper floor have fine views: Room 6 features vistas of Fisherman Bay and has a fireplace and sitting area. New owners Maryanne Miller and Clark Haley serve breakfast at individual tables in the dining room. The only B&B on the island to accept children, it is also walking distance to the restaurants and shops in town. *132 Lopez Rd (Lopez Village, right in town), PO Box 271, Lopez Island, WA 98261; 360/468-3238; edenwildinn@msn.com; www.edenwildinn.com; $$$; AE, MC, V; checks OK.*

FISHERMAN BAY GUEST HOUSE

 It's just one very large room with a bathroom, and over a garage at that, but it has a killer view of Fisherman Bay and the channel beyond the bay—and it's loaded with extras: a woodstove, interesting kitchen stuff, homemade sweet breads and organic coffee for breakfast, popcorn for the microwave, a comfy queen bed, handmade soaps in the bath—even a stack of romantic CDs. There's a big deck that catches the afternoon sun and a little trail through the pretty garden to a couple of bone-bleached driftwood logs on a scrap of beach on the bay. Very nice indeed. Ask owner Jan Lewis, who lives in the old yellow farmhouse next door, about her condo (one bedroom, two baths) for rent in Lopez Village. *2612 Fisherman Bay Rd, Lopez Island, WA 98261; 360/468-2884; $$; MC, V; checks OK.*

INN AT SWIFTS BAY

The most appealing accommodation on Lopez is this handsome Tudor inn, formerly a summer home, set among the cedars above Swifts Bay. Though new innkeepers were just finding their feet as we visited, they appear committed to maintaining the fine blend of pampering guests and letting them be, which has established the inn's reputation for a decade. Public rooms are cozy and charming. Choose from two large, comfortable bedrooms (with shared bath) or three suites (with gas log fireplaces and private baths). Our favorite, the Red Cabbage Suite, is a very private space with a separate sitting area, an afternoon-sun deck, and a VCR and CD stereo sound system. There's also a secluded outdoor hot tub that can be scheduled for private sittings (towels, robes, and slippers provided), a first-class selection of movies on tape, and a tiny exercise studio with a two-person sauna. You will need it after breakfast, an elegant presentation of fruit, home-baked pastries, and an elaborate entrée that might range from salmon potato cakes to a Brie and

For a home of your own, contact Barbara Pickering at Island House Realty, 360/468-3401 or 360/468-3366. She manages vacation rentals—from small cottages and farmhouses to a home with a private beach to a house on 40 acres of land at Iceberg Point (about $1,800 a week). Also check the bulletin board at Lopez Island Market for Lopez rentals.

apple omelet. The windswept bay is a five-minute walk away. *856 Port Stanley Rd (head 1 mile south of ferry to Port Stanley Rd, left 1 mile), Lopez Island, WA 98261; 360/468-3636; inn@swiftsbay.com; www.swiftsbay.com; $$$; AE, DIS, MC, V; checks OK.*

THE ISLAND FARMHOUSE

Aside from campsites, this 12-acre working farm is the only resting spot that's much of a deal on Lopez. Owners Ted and Susan Sanchez have added a large room off the back of their home, with its own deck and private entry. It is generous in size and decorated à la Laura Ashley. The private bath is quite large, and there's a kitchen nook. Sit on your deck in the morning and watch the sheepdog at work on the herd of Suffolks in this pastoral setting. There's also a cabin under the apple trees. *Hummel Lake Rd, PO Box 3114, Lopez Island, WA 98261; 360/468-2864; $; no credit cards; checks OK.*

LOPEZ FARM COTTAGES ★

Amid sheep and cedars on 30 acres of prime Lopez pastureland, John and Ann Warsen built four cozy (read: tiny) cottages and fitted them with stylish pine interiors and plenty of windows. Each has a gas fireplace, a queen-size bed, front and back porches, and a minikitchen (fridge, microwave, sink, and dishes), making them suitable for extended getaways. But they're not bad for weekend romance either, with double-headed showers in every bathroom and a basket of fixings for continental breakfast plus ground coffee delivered each evening for the next morning. The Warsens are gracious hosts. Unless you're from Iowa, the field setting may lack a feeling of landscape, but the acreage is a work in progress: campsites have been added in the cedar grove, and there's a large and private hot tub for cottage guest use. Everyone parks in a central lot. A cart is provided to take provisions and luggage down paved and graveled pathways to campsites and cottages. *555 Fisherman Bay Rd (2 7/10 miles from ferry), Lopez Island, WA 98261; 800/440-3556 or 360/468-3555; $$$; MC, V; checks OK.*

MACKAYE HARBOR INN ★

Location, location, location. Bicyclists call it paradise after their sweaty trek from the ferry to this little harbor. The tall powder-blue house, built in 1927, sits above a sandy, shell-strewn beach, perfect for sunset strolls or pushing off in one of their rented kayaks to explore the scenic waterways. The Harbor Suite is our top choice, with its fireplace, private bath, and enclosed sitting area facing the beach. Rent kayaks or borrow mountain bikes, ask the very friendly innkeepers, Mike and Robin Bergstrom, to share their secrets about the island, and you're off to explore. Return in the afternoon for freshly baked cookies. If you do come by bike, be warned: the closest restaurant is 6 miles back in town. Breakfast gets you started before a long morning of paddling out to the otters. Mountain bikes are free to guests; kayak rates for guests are the lowest price in the islands ($25 a day or $35 for the entire stay). *949 MacKaye Harbor Rd (12 miles south of ferry landing), Lopez Island, WA 98261; 360/468-2253; $$; MC, V; checks OK.*

LUMMI ISLAND

Located just off Gooseberry Point northwest of Bellingham, Lummi is one of the most overlooked islands of the ferry-accessible San Juans. It echoes the days when the San Juan Islands were still a hidden treasure, visited only by folks who preferred bucolic surroundings and deserted beaches to a plethora of restaurants and gift shops. Private ownership has locked up most of this pastoral isle, so you won't find state parks or resorts. To stretch your limbs, bring bikes and enjoy the quiet country roads. Plan ahead; dining options tend to be seasonal.

Lummi is serviced not by Washington State Ferries but by the tiny Whatcom County ferry, which leaves Gooseberry Point about 10 minutes past the hour from 6am until midnight (more frequently on weekdays). It's easy to find (just follow the signs to Lummi Island from I-5, north of Bellingham), cheap ($4 round trip for a car and two passengers), and quick (a 6-minute crossing); call ahead for schedule, 360/676-6730. The ferry returns from Lummi on the hour.

ACTIVITIES

Beach Combing. On steep-banked Lummi Island, many of the best beaches are accessible only by boat or kayak. Most are Department of Natural Resources sites on the island's east side. One beach accessible by trail (staircase, actually) is DNR Beach 224, which extends north about 100 yards from the ferry landing. Park at the landing and walk north along the road to a viewing platform, where stairs lead down.

Boating. Shorelines and secluded coves around Lummi Island are ripe for boat exploration. Favorites include Inati Bay on the southeast side of the island (two mooring buoys, picnic facilities) and nearby DNR Beaches 223, 223A, and 223B, all of which have sandy landings. Most other DNR beaches on Lummi Island are rocky, some of them very hazardous for all but kayakers.

Lummi Island also serves as a launching point for ventures into the small, lesser known islands in the San Juan chain. Nestled between Lummi and Bellingham on the mainland, they make nice day trips by boat. Eliza, Vendovi, and Sinclair Islands ring the southern end of Lummi. The largest and westernmost, Sinclair, has a public dock and beach access on the south end. Tiny Vendovi has public tidelands access all the way around, below the high-tide line. Uplands are private, but some nice coves await boaters in small craft. Eliza isn't well suited for beach landings and is mostly private land.

A public boat launch is available at Legoe Bay, on the northwest side of Lummi Island. Avoid it in bad weather, however; it's rather exposed. In addition, a launch hoist is available at Gooseberry Point, near the Lummi Island ferry landing.

Kayaking. Lummi Island's many secluded DNR beaches make fine kayak destinations. One of them, Lummi Island Recreation Site, near Reil Harbor on the southeast side of the island, is a designated beachside campsite for the state's Cascadia Marine Trail (a state-managed water trail including campsites from Olympia to Vancouver, BC; 206/545-9161; wwta@eskimo.com; www.wwta.org). Note: No running water.

Hiking. A popular hike leads from a Seacrest Drive trailhead to the top of Lummi Peak which has grand views of the San Juans and the North Sound. This moderate hike is 7 miles round trip. Warning: The trail is hard to follow at the top, so be careful along the cliffs.

Biking. Road riders love the 7-mile triangular loop around the north end of Lummi Island; start at the Lummi ferry dock and follow Nugent Road, West Shore Drive, and Legoe Bay Road. It's moderately hilly. Bicycle rentals are available at the store next to The Islander, a few yards from the ferry landing.

Wildlife. There are plenty of chances to rub binocular lenses with wild animals on Lummi Island. Marine wildlife lovers may see migratory birds such as loons and numerous duck species passing by. A popular marine mammal haunt— great for whale watchers and seabird lovers—is the west side of the island, including the rocks and small islands just off the shore. Most are protected portions of the San Juan Island National Wildlife Refuge.

GETTING THERE

To reach Lummi Island, drive north on I-5 to exit 260, follow-
ing Slater Road west. Turn left (southwest) on Haxton Way, and
follow it to the Lummi Island ferry, 360/676-6730. Sailings are
hourly, and the crossing of Hales Pass takes about 6 minutes.

LODGINGS

THE WILLOWS INN

Run as a resort since the late 1920s, the old Taft family house perches on a knoll 100 feet above the accessible beach, offering sweeping views of the San Juan and Gulf Islands. There is a small cottage for two with a kitchen (decor is a bit precious, but the view and privacy are terrific), and a two-bedroom guest house that looks out over the rose garden to the ocean (with a little of the kitchen roof in between). For couples traveling together, the last is our favorite; it also boasts a gas fireplace and a Jacuzzi. The innkeepers don't serve any meals, but full kitchens are available in the cottage and the guest house. *2579 W Shore Dr (from ferry, north on Nugent for 3H miles), Lummi Island, WA 98262; 360/758-2620; willows@lummi-island.com; www. lummi-island.com/willows; $$$; MC, V; checks OK.*

GULF
ISLANDS

GULF ISLANDS

The Gulf Islands stretch along the Strait of Georgia, between Vancouver Island and the British Columbia mainland. Similar in geography and philosophy to Washington's San Juan Islands, the Gulf Islands also enjoy the same rain-shadow weather and offer wonderful boating and cycling opportunities. While there are literally hundreds of these islands, only a handful are inhabited. They are less developed than the San Juan Islands, and have much more public land—there are at least 60 marine parks in the Gulf Islands, compared to the 11 in the San Juan Islands. Salt Spring Island is the largest and most densely populated of the Gulf Islands, with about 10,000 year-round residents and an economy driven by tourism. The Outer Islands (the term used to describe all of the other islands) are more sparsely settled, with populations that range from a high of about 4,000 (Gabriola) to a low of around 300 (Saturna).

"We like the community events like the Fall Fair or the Halloween bonfire, and we go to all the concerts. There's a real sense of excitement and belonging when you just mill around with the crowd, watching friends and neighbors meet up with each other."
—Michelle and Jonathan Grant, island residents

ACTIVITIES

Camping. Provincial campgrounds (operated and reserved through BC Parks, 250/391-2300) are probably the best deals going on the islands. Most have water, firewood, and separate areas for tent campers. Summer is drought season on all of the islands, and water is at a premium during these months, when forests and meadows are tinder-dry and highly combustible. Therefore campfires and outdoor cooking are prohibited in many campsites. To avoid the summer crunch, arrive early; only some of the campgrounds have spillover areas.

Galiano: Along with the beaches, hiking, and educational opportunities, Montague Harbour Marine Provincial Park also has 40 wooded campsites just off the beach. These are reservable sites, and we recommend that you do. Nearby is a marina with a seasonal store, where groceries and supplies may be purchased. Dionisio Point Provincial Park has 30 sites but marine access only, few amenities are offered.

North Pender: Prior Centennial Provincial Park has 17 campsites. And for those who like to camp but don't want to cook, the campground is convenient to the pub. Reservable sites.

From Crofton (mid-Vancouver Island, about 60 kilometers north of Victoria), you can take a ferry to Vesuvius Bay, on the north end of Salt Spring. The Crofton-Vesuvius ferry runs more or less hourly, takes about 20 minutes, and is seldom as crowded as either the Long Harbour or Fulford ferries.

GETTING THERE

Via Ferry. BC Ferries provides relatively frequent and easy access to all of the major islands from Tsawwassen and Horseshoe Bay on the mainland, and Nanaimo, Crofton, and Swartz Bay (near Sidney) on Vancouver Island. The ferries can be crowded, particularly during summer months and on holiday weekends.

If you plan to bring a vehicle, you can book a prepaid reservation to the Gulf Islands by phoning BC Ferries at 888/223-3779 from BC only or, from the United States, 250/386-3431. From late May through September, one- and two-hour sailing waits are not uncommon.

Pay your fare at any terminal with cash, Visa or MasterCard. Once on board the ferry, you'll need cash for the newsstand and cafeteria. It's also worth noting that bank services and ATMs on the Outer Islands are rare; several islands have neither a bank nor a bank machine.

Ferry service can run up to $35.50 (Canadian) for your car, $9 for the driver and $9 for each additional passenger one way, with lower return fares. Prices go up each year. Inter-island ferries are less expensive, but the cost does add up. Walk-on is

South Pender: Beaumont Marine Provincial Park, 11 tent sites, access from the water or hike over the hill from Mount Norman.

Salt Spring: Ruckle Provincial Park offers 78 tent sites with picnic tables (the best are the waterfront sites). On weekends things can get tight, and on long weekends the place is crammed. No restaurants are nearby, so bring provisions.

 Marine Parks. There are private marinas and government docks (marked with red paint along the railings) at each of the Gulf Islands. But boaters will also find excellent moorage at any of the 60 or more marine parks that dot the BC shorelines and islands from Prince Rupert to Galiano Island. Recently, more than $60 million was approved for additional purchase of Crown Land and private property to create a virtual necklace of public land throughout the islands. Following *always the cheapest rate. Pay attention to the schedules to make sure the ferry you're on actually stops at your desired destination.*

Forget the Car. Given the expense, and inconvenience of ferry lines, alternative transportation methods deserve serious consideration. Foot passengers and bicyclists seldom encounter problems with sailing waits. Bicyclists pay the same fare on BC Ferries as walk-on passengers. Most bed-and-breakfast hosts will arrange to meet guests at the ferries. Hitchhiking is, so far, relatively safe and socially acceptable on all of the islands, but limited traffic means you should be prepared to hike some distance to your destination. Bicycle touring is an increasingly popular method of experiencing the islands, but would-be cyclists should be aware that many island roads are steep, twisty, and narrow with no shoulders.

Or Fly. You can also try the island airlines. The cost typically runs about $130 per person to Ganges Harbour on Salt Spring, either from Vancouver International Airport or from Vancouver's harbor, at the foot of Denman Street. For fares and schedules, contact Pacific Spirit Air, 800/665-2359 or 250/537-9359 or Harbour Air Seaplanes., 800/665-0212 or 604/688-1277.

are descriptions of a few marine parks that are on the smaller islands—those that aren't accessed by BC Ferries.

Newcastle Island: This island in Nanaimo Harbour has a colorful history. Originally inhabited by the Salish people, as were all the islands in both the San Juan and Gulf Islands, it has since been the site of a coal mine, a sandstone quarry, a shipyard, and, in the years before the Second World War, a luxury resort owned by Canadian Pacific Steamships Ltd. The pavilion from that era has been restored and now houses a dance floor, restaurant, and snack bar. There are bays, beaches, playing fields, and more than 20 kilometers of trails and 500 meters of mooring floats. During the summer, a passenger ferry runs between Nanaimo and the island.

Pirates Cove: This popular marine park is at the southeast tip of De Courcy Island. The dock to the starboard of the entry is private. There are dinghy floats, trails (including one to Ruxton Beach), camping, picnicking, toilets, and drinking water.

Additional anchorage is available at Whaleboat Island Provincial Marine Park, nearby.

Princess Margaret (Portland Island): Between Satellite Channel and Prevost Passage, just southeast of Salt Spring, this island was named in honor of HRH Princess Margaret's visit to BC in 1958. Numerous shoals and reefs around the island dictate care in approaching it. Sandy beaches stretch along the northwest and southwest shores, and there are fair-weather anchorages at Royal Cove and Princess Bay. Facilities include toilets, water, and camping and picnicking facilities, as well as a network of walking trails.

Sidney Spit: At the northern tip of Sidney Island, between Miners Channel and Sidney Channel, lies this sheltered anchorage, with thousands of meters of beach for swimming, sunbathing, and beachcombing. Seasonal landing floats are available for small craft. Camping and picnicking facilities, water, toilets, play areas, and walking trails, as well as passenger service from Sidney in the summer.

Wallace Island: In Trincomali Channel between Salt Spring and Galiano Islands, this narrow island offers picturesque, sheltered anchorages at Princess Cove and Conover Cove. Numerous reefs and shoals require a cautious approach. Camping and picnicking facilities, drinking water, and toilets are available, and there's a dock at Conover Cove. Fires are prohibited. Be considerate of the two private properties on the island.

WATER TAXIS

Short of cruising in a private vessel, water taxis provide the most convenient (though expensive) method of island-hopping. Gulf Island Water Taxi, 250/537-2510, has a fleet of 5 boats (also available for charters) that can carry up to 50 passengers, plus luggage, supplies, and bikes. In the summers, scheduled runs are made between Galiano, Mayne, and Salt Spring Islands for $15 round trip—a great way to see the islands. Coffee and treats are served on board.

Viable Marine Services (Box 45, Saturna, BC V0N 2Y0, 250/539-3200) offers water taxi services to Vancouver Island's Swartz Bay, and they'll pick you up from and return you to any of the southern Gulf Islands, and can also transport bicycles or kayaks. Dress warmly.

SALT SPRING ISLAND

Salt Spring is the largest and most diverse of the Gulf Islands, as well as the most developed. Yet it manages to maintain much of its rural character: sheep outnumber artists and their flock of galleries.

On Salt Spring, all roads lead to Ganges, where islanders are headed when they say they're going into town. Here, you'll find all the usual urban amenities, including banks (and three ATMs), the liquor store, restaurants, the Saturday Market, two good bakeries, grocery stores, and a cluster of galleries. Though Ganges may be the island's commercial center, laid-back Fulford is the cultural hub.

You see, the island has a split personality. The south end (where you'll find Fulford) is what people usually mean when they think of Salt Spring. It is a quiet, rural, workaday area, with rolling meadows and lush old orchards. In Fulford, the calendar stalled somewhere around 1972. But that's the magic of the place, and no one seems to notice, or much mind, the anachronism. The north end (where you'll find Ganges) is more densely populated and gentrified. But at either end, the social code is relaxed; the scruffy hippie next to you in the pub could very well be the owner of that yacht with the on-board helicopter pad.

> "The thing I love about Salt Spring is its incredible versatility. On a typical fall day, I can harvest wheat in the morning, swim in the ocean in the afternoon, then listen to jazz at Moby's in the evening. I can hang out with the counterculture types at Barb's Buns, go up Mount Tuam and be a Buddhist, or sip cappuccino with the yuppies in Ganges."
> —Dave Phillips, a Salt Spring businessman

ACTIVITIES

Marinas. Salt Spring has plenty of places for boaters to tie up for a night or two. In Ganges Harbour you'll find such amenities as fuel, groceries, water, power hookups, marine and fishing supplies, showers, and laundry. Try Ganges Marina, 250/537-5242, or Salt Spring Marina, 250/537-5810. On the south end of the island is Fulford Harbour Marina, 250/653-4467, which offers similar amenities.

For short-term tie-ups, try the government docks (they're marked with bright red trim) at Fernwood Point, Ganges Harbour, Fulford Harbour, Musgrave Landing, Burgoyne Bay, and Vesuvius Bay. There's no overnight moorage at these docks, and fishing boats have priority.

 Historic Park. Ruckle Provincial Park, which abuts Beaver Point Provincial Park at the southernmost edge of

GETTING THERE

Geographically, Salt Spring can be divided into three parts, marked conveniently by the three ferry terminals: Long Harbour (east side), Fulford (south end), and Vesuvius Bay (north end). The largest of these, and closest to the commercial center of Ganges, is Long Harbour. If you arrive from Tsawwassen on BC's mainland, or from any of the Outer Islands, this is where you'll disembark.

An alternative that will give you greater control over your arrival time is to take BC Ferries from Tsawwassen to Swartz Bay on Vancouver Island, and then pick up an inter-island ferry from Swartz Bay to Fulford on Salt Spring. The Tsawwassen–Swartz Bay ferries run frequently during the summer months and less often September to May; crossing time is 2½ hours. They are large and comfortable, with well-stocked newsstands, and the trip takes you through some of the most spectacular scenery in the world. Pods of orcas are frequent escorts, as are eagles.

The ferry from Swartz Bay to Fulford Harbour runs about every 90 minutes and take about a half hour. When you buy your ticket at Tsawwassen, be sure to ask for a through-fare to Fulford. You won't actually save time or money, but you can at least plan your arrival on Salt Spring at your convenience. This ricochet-run also works with the Outer Islands, although the connecting ferries aren't as frequent.

Salt Spring, combines a private, working farm with public parkland. The farm was built in 1872, and it's the oldest in British Columbia (inland BC land was not cultivated until irrigation systems were built). Descendants of the Ruckle family, the original settlers, donated their home and lands to the provincial government. They still live in the charming, gingerbread Victorian farmhouse located at the park gates, and their sheep graze in the meadows that surround it. Public roads and trails meander around and through the gently rolling, bucolic landscape, out to the sprawling, sandstone beaches. You walk from the parking lot through an orchard and enter the weathered old barn where farm machinery is displayed, then walk around the original farmhouse and several old outbuildings. And you can buy vegetables and flowers from several roadside stands adjacent to the family's houses. Beaver Point Hall, an old community hall, marks the starting point for a hike to Ruckle Provincial Park.

Snacks. Visit the Bouzouki Cafe in Grace Point Square in Ganges for hearty, Greek-style food; 250/537-4181. Just across the way is Alfresco's, 250/537-5979, which offers great soups and sandwiches and Italian-influenced entrees in the street-level cafe. Coffee addicts can get their latte fix at either the chocoholic's mecca called Harlan's, 250/537-4434, or Moka House, 250/537-1216.

Island History. Bob Ackerman's museum, housed in a log cabin near Fulford, is dedicated to his Cowichan grandmother who married into the pioneer Ackerman family in the 1860s. (It may be more accurate to say that the Ackermans married into the Cowichans, a matriarchal Coast Salish tribe.) Over the years the Ackerman family found many artifacts on Salt Spring beaches—arrowheads, spear points, stone pipes, fish clubs, and net weights—and they are displayed here, along with other things collected, such as rain hats made of woven cedar bark, reed mats, and handmade clothing. A photograph shows a longhouse built on what is today part of the Tsowat Band's Reserve on the south end of the island. To see the little museum and get a personal tour, call 250/653-4228. Free.

Some of the oldest and most picturesque buildings on Salt Spring Island are its churches, including the much-photographed, lovely stone St. Paul's Roman Catholic Church (1880) overlooking Fulford Harbour, and nearby wood frame St. Mary's Anglican Church on the Fulford-Ganges Road. A church pamphlet at the Information Centre in Ganges lists services and has a map.

Swimming. St. Mary Lake, at the north end of Salt Spring, is the largest in the Gulf Islands. Although there are no public beaches, this is a favored spot among the locals for swimming and freshwater fishing. The best accesses are on private property (mostly belonging to the resorts that dot its eastern edge). There are also little pockets of access on Tripp Road, on the west side of the lake, and on North End Road, but you have to be

The ferry from Tsawwassen to Long Harbour on Salt Spring Island is the one most likely to leave you stranded in the parking lot during the high tourist season. There are just a few sailings a day, each taking about two and a half hours, and the last Friday sailing is notoriously late, commonly delivering you long after the scheduled midnight arrival.

keen-eyed to spot them. The Tripp Road access is at the very end of the road; the North End Road access is just to the south of the water treatment plant. These are not marked, but should be identifiable by the presence of other swimmers. No gas-powered boats are allowed on St. Mary or on any of four other island lakes. While there are a few beaches on Salt Spring, saltwater swimming is a pleasure best reserved for the most sultry of summer days. If you are determined to swim in salt water, go to the beach near Vesuvius Bay at the foot of Langley Road.

Bike Rentals. Many B&Bs provide complimentary bicycles for their guests. You can also rent an island bike from Salt Spring Marine Rentals at Moby's Marina, 250/537-9100. Salt Spring Kayaking on the public dock at Fulford also rents bikes; 250/653-4222.

Saturday Market. The not-to-be-missed social event of the week is Salt Spring's Saturday Market, held outdoors around the perimeter of Centennial Park in downtown Ganges, rain or shine, every Saturday from about the first of April to the end of October. At its height in midsummer, the market has as many as 50 vendors, selling everything imaginable, from homemade preserves and organic vegetables to healing crystals and tie-dyed T-shirts. It's as much a cultural activity as a shopping experience.

Shopping. The most readily identifiable building in Ganges is Mouat's Mall, not to be confused with a conventional suburban shopping center. Mouat's is the big, rickety white-and-green building on the waterfront. The first and second floors contain a well-stocked hardware store (where you can pick up camping equipment, fishing tackle and licenses, and any other necessity you may have left behind), with a not-bad housewares and kitchen section upstairs. At the rear of the mall, in a corrugated metal annex, is the tiny Volume Two Bookstore, 250/537-9223, which has an impressive selection of local histories, charts and maps, crafts books, and classics of Canadian literature. In the lower level you'll find Pegasus Gallery of Canadian Art, 250/537-2421, with some of the finest local art around; there's also a splendid representation of Northwest native arts here, including the work of some of British Columbia's finest totem and mask

Stuff & Nonsense, just up the road from the Fulford ferry terminal, is the place to go for funky all-natural clothing for kids and adults, wild hats, and gadgets and gizmos of all sorts. Believe it or not, there's nothing too pricey here, and lots that will give you change from a $20 bill (2909 Fulford-Ganges Road, Fulford, 250/653-4620).

Salt Spring Island has a bus service that, for a very reasonable cost, will get you just about anywhere you want to go. The buses, which take the scenic route, run from Ruckle Provincial Park at the south end to North Beach Road at the north end, with convenient stops along the way, including one at the entrance to the Cusheon Creek Hostel. The buses meet all ferries, except the late-evening ferry at Long Harbour. Cyclists and backpackers can stash their gear in the buses' capacious cargo compartments.

You can rent virtually any form of transportation imaginable in Ganges Heritage Car & Truck Rentals, in the Harbour Building, 250/537-4225, rents cars and scooters.

carvers. Finally, the Boardwalk Cafe, 250/537-5747, will revive you with a cappuccino and a pastry or a bowl of homemade soup.

French Country Fabric Creations (109 Broadwell Road, 250/537-9865) is a lovely little house, modeled on Marie Antoinette's Versailles hideaway. Owner Darlene Lane specializes in small, impeccably crafted household items, handbags sewn from Provence-patterned cottons, and delicate laces from Portugal.

Goings On. On January 1st, visit Vesuvius Beach for the Polar Bear Swim. You don't really have to go swimming, but it's surprising how many people do. This is mostly a spectator sport, with everybody gathering at the Vesuvius Inn for hot chocolate afterward. September brings the annual Fall Fair at the Farmer's Institute, and fun for the whole family. Tip: There's likely to be a parking spot or two vacant in the cement works yard next to the institute.

Arts and Crafts. Salt Spring has a well-deserved reputation as a center for arts and crafts, from fine, all-natural soaps and perfumes to funky, folk-art birdhouses to herbal concoctions of all sorts. Many artisans open their studios to the public; there is a self-conducted studio tour April to October on Sundays (11am–4pm). The map is available through the Tourist Information Centre and at galleries. Watch for road signs marked with the word "studio" and two black sheep, indicating an open

The pottery at Judy Weeden Studio (125 Primrose Lane, 250/537-5403), embellished with glazed botanic and symbolic motifs, is sophisticated and beautifully executed.

Great Expectations (116 Collins Road, 250/537-4146) shows off lots of weavings, great gift ideas (including do-it-yourself dried-flower wreaths), and Jonathan Grant's spectacular wildlife photography.

studio. You can see selected artists' studios with Salt Spring Tours, 250/537-4737, about a three-hour Sunday excursion that stops at between five to eight studios for about $20 per person.

Ute Hagen Studio (180 Hedger Road, 250/537-4812) is a must-see, both for the old, heritage-farm setting and for Hagen's vibrant paintings and exquisite terra-cotta tiles, inspired by the colors and cultures of Mexico.

Plan to be awestruck by the sheer volume and variety of dried flowers, and the number of arrangements available, at Everlasting Summer (194 McLennan Drive, 250/653-9418). Spend some time exploring the many little gardens that surround the studio. (This is also a good starting point for a day hike through Beaver Point Park.)

Gary and Beth Cherneff live and work in an absolutely magical setting of forest, ferns, and ocean views. Especially noteworthy are Gary's terra-cotta planters, while Beth's dried flower arrangements are imaginative and unusual. Check them out at their studio, Stoneridge Pottery (520 Long Harbour Road, 250/537-9252).

The Waterfront Gallery (107 Purvis Lane, 250/537-4525) offers one of the best assortments of crafts on any of the islands, from pottery and woven blankets to handcrafted teddy bears made from vintage fur coats. In Grace Point Square (around the corner from Mouat's Mall) are the Naikai Gallery, 250/537-4400, and the Thunderbird Gallery, 250/537-1144, both worth a browse for high-quality fine art and crafts. The island's best collection of fine art by local artists is at Pegasus Gallery of Canadian Art, 250/537-2421, in Mouat's Mall.

Horseback Riding. Salt Spring Guided Rides, 250/537-5761, offers guided tours on horseback through quiet, picturesque farmland and forests. The owners have been conducting these tours for more than 10 years, and are adept at matching horse to rider. Phone for reservations (no drop-ins) at least a week or two in advance during the summer.

Performing Arts. Touring artists of international stature, such as Loreena McKennitt, Liona Boyd, and the Quarteto Gelato, frequently visit the island, an experience made even more attractive by Ganges' new multipurpose performing arts center, ArtSpring (call for events, 250/537-2125).

The island's other facilities lack in acoustics, but that's more than compensated for by the intimacy of a small hall and a genuinely enthusiastic audience. On any weekend there's likely to be a choice of performances by any one of a dozen local choirs, theater groups, or dance troupes. Concerts and plays are still performed in the local high school gymnasium or at Mahon Hall, Ganges' all-purpose community hall, when ArtSpring is booked. For up-to-date information on who's playing where, check the *Driftwood*, the island's community newspaper, published weekly.

The pubs host open stages on selected nights, and each attracts a different style of music. Moby's Marine Pub, 250/537-5559, opens its stage on Wednesdays for alternative music, and Sunday evenings are given over to jazz. Classic rock and dance music fans might enjoy karaoke nights at Harbour House Bistro, 250/537-4700, or acoustic folk rock at Vesuvius Inn, 250/537-2312. Vesuvius Inn, a sharp left turn from the Vesuvius ferry dock, at the end of Vesuvius Bay Road, commands one of the best views on the island—particularly from the wraparound verandah, and especially at sunset. The food is good, if you like pub food, the atmosphere is welcoming, and the locals really do hang out here. (That Chernobyl-like structure across Sansum Narrows is the Crofton pulp mill. If you notice a heavy, sweetish odor thick enough to gag a goat, that's the source. Fortunately, these rare emissions usually dissipate by late morning.)

Fishing. For saltwater fishing, Sansum Narrows (the body of water between Vancouver Island and Salt Spring) is one of the area's best fishing grounds for chinook and coho salmon. Trincomali Channel (between Salt Spring and Galiano Islands) is another favorite, as is Houston Passage, off Southey Point. Cod are found off Fernwood Point and at Isabella Island. Pick up a copy of the annual BC Fishing Guide to check on regulations, permitted sizes, and times of year when fishing is legal. You can charter a fishing trip with Something Fishy (at Salt Spring Marina, 250/537-9100) with gear and bait supplied, or rent one of their powerboats (two-hour minimum). Tackle rentals, bait, and provisions are available through Salt Spring Marina (120 Upper Ganges Road, 250/537-5810).

Several of Salt Spring's lakes boast excellent freshwater fishing, particularly for cutthroat trout and smallmouth bass. No

You can pick up the Sunday New York Times *(a week or so late), the* Manchester Guardian, *or any number of British tabs that will keep you in touch with the lives and loves of assorted royals, at Parkside News, Ganges, 250/537-2812.*

gas-powered boats are allowed on any of the lakes—rowboats or electric motors only. Cedar Beach Resort (1136 North End Road, 250/537-2205) on the north end of St. Mary Lake has boats and fishing gear for rent. St. Mary Lake is well stocked with smallmouth bass and rainbow and cutthroat trout. Blackburn Lake has cutthroat and bass from spring through fall. Access is off a small lane west of the Fulford-Ganges Road, just north of Horel Road. Cusheon Lake has cutthroat trout from spring through fall. Stowell and Weston Lakes have cutthroat and rainbow trout from spring through fall.

 Hiking. Walking along quiet country roads is one of the great pleasures of rural life. To avoid infringing on anyone's privacy, stick to the paved roads or pick up a copy of the Salt Spring Out-of-Doors map. The Salt Spring Trail and Nature Club has been seeking out and marking a network of trails that (they hope) will eventually transect the whole island. To date, they've mapped three of the most popular hiking areas, with more to come. Please carry out anything you carry in, leave your dog at home (trails meander along many pastures with sheep and other livestock), and be sure to tread carefully. Trail maps are available at the Salt Spring Chamber of Commerce in Ganges, 250/537-4223.

"Salt Spring offers me a scale of life I can deal with. There are a million walks to take, a million coves to explore, and all the time in the world to do it in."
—Scott Hyland, actor

Duck Creek Park trail follows a tree-lined creek into an open meadow, about a 45-minute walk on 14 acres, located between Broadwell Road and Sunset Drive. Dunbabin Park's 7 acres of large cedars and firs offer a trail along the creek, about a 20-minute walk. You get there off Robinson and Stark Roads. A better workout is at Fern Creek Park, along a deep gorge carpeted with ferns. Enter off Isabella Point Road, south of Drummond Park. Mouat Park's 55 acres is a network of hiking trails; entrance is on Seaview Drive just past ArtSpring. Peter Arnell Park's trail meanders through the forest to astounding viewpoints overlooking Galiano Island and Active Pass.

Southey Point offers an easy half-day stroll through the woods (with a few steep parts) to a lovely, wide beach. Look for the red marker on the east side of Southey Point Road, just a few meters off Sunset Drive.

The hike up Mount Erskine is mostly moderate, with a steep climb to the peak. Allow an hour and a half each way. Pink tape marks the start of the trail on the east side of Collins Road, just off Rainbow Road. The views at the top are of the Maxwell Creek Valley and across Sansum Narrows to Vancouver Island.

Exploring Mount Maxwell is an easy half-day hike. Drive up Cranberry Ridge to Maxwell Road (which gets a bit rough near the top). Pick up the trails from the parking lot, and allow several hours to explore the whole network. Take in the deep peace of an old-growth coniferous forest and spectacular cliff-top views of the Gulf Islands; keep a lookout for bald eagles.

Beaver Point Provincial Park and Ruckle Provincial Park both provide easy walking tours for the whole family. Allow several hours—at least a half day—for explorations. Pick up the trail behind Beaver Point Hall or Beaver Point School. At the northeast corner of the park, another trail leads into Ruckle Park, one of the most delightful areas on Salt Spring. The trails are easy to walk, and easy to follow. You'll pass through old-growth stands of cedar, fir, hemlock, and maple; see an abundance of wildflowers; and maybe catch sight of an orca or two from the beach.

A challenging climb up a primitive switchback road takes you to the dramatic vistas at the peak of Mount Tuam. Follow Isabella Point Road to Mountain Road on the right. Depending on your vehicle—four-wheel drive is best—you can drive up about 3½ kilometers to an old logging road. Park here, then follow this road

The drive from Vesuvius Bay out to Southey Point takes you through some of the most gorgeous scenery— acres and acres of meadows, populated mostly by sheep, Salt Spring's most famous export. Follow Sunset Drive (off Vesuvius Bay Road) to Southey Point Road.

"A perfect day would be to start at the Saturday Market, then go up Mount Maxwell, and end up with dinner at one of the waterfront restaurants."
—Dave Phillips, island resident

to the right. Watch for cairns marking the way. Plan a full day for this one.

Beach Walking. Walker Hook is one of Salt Spring's most interesting geographical features. Almost an island, it is accessible only by private boat—the land connection is private property—but for those who make the effort, the payoff is a lovely, sandy beach, reputedly the best on the island.

Another small beach can be reached by Beddis Road. This may be the prettiest road on the island, once you're past the light industrial section. (From Ganges, take the Fulford-Ganges Road, and turn right onto Beddis Road.) The road winds around old farms, forest, and ocean shoreline, and finally culminates in a little maze of streets. At the end of Beddis, look for Lionel Street and follow it down to the beach. Like all of the island's public beaches, this one is not well marked, and it's easy to miss. Once there, your reward is a sheltered little pebble beach with spectacular views across Trincomali Channel. The beach, surrounded by spectacular private properties, is small and likely to be crowded during the summer.

Welbury Bay Park is just 1 acre, but it has a low bank (easy access) with southwest exposure—great for a picnic and swimming. It's adjacent to Long Harbour Ferry off Scott Point Drive. The path is marked by two rock cairns.

At Vesuvius Bay, a trail leads down to a sandy beachfront park, about a 10-minute hike. This is a nice place for tidal pools at low tide.

Drummond Park, which faces east at Fulford Harbour, is under trees, but has a nice sandy beach to explore, with tide pools at low tide. The island's only publicized petroglyph is enshrined here.

Movies. For cinema buffs, Salt Spring boasts a small movie theater, Salt Spring Cinema, 250/537-4656, in Central Hall at the junction where Vesuvius Bay Road meets Lower Ganges and Upper Ganges Roads. While the selection is limited, the films are always recent releases. The theater owner frequently brings in foreign and art-house films, and marks Canada Day every year with a weeklong festival of Canadian films. Tuesday nights are half price.

Picnics. For island ingredients for a home-cooked meal or a picnic, check out the Creekside Building in Ganges, a low-slung, West Coast wonder of cedar and glass. Here you'll find Mobile Market, 250/537-1784, offering the best choice of fruits and vegetables on the island. Much of the produce is organic and locally grown.

In the same building is Barb's Buns, 250/537-4491, a favorite local hangout where the breads and pastries are always fresh and delicious, and frequently organic. Across the street, Salt Spring Roasting Company offers organic coffee to go; 250/537-0825. Fish lovers will appreciate The Fishery, 250/537-2457, on Rainbow Road overlooking the harbor. It's fisherman-owned and serves up Pacific salmon, live crab, and smoked fish. Check out the Salt Spring Dairy on Upper Ganges Road, 250/537-1300, for Avalon ice cream, goat and sheep's cheeses, farm-fresh eggs, honey, and garlic.

Knoth's Fine Foods (1320 North Beach Road, 250/537-9760), which is open only weekdays after 5pm (the owners all have day jobs) and on weekends, offers free-range, organically grown meats such as chicken, rabbit, Muscovy duck, and lamb. In addition to their own homegrown meats, they sell bratwurst prepared according to a traditional family recipe, as well as locally caught and smoked wild salmon and fresh seafoods. Island deer hunters can bring their trophies to Knoth's for butchering and to have the meat ground into sausage.

Farm and Garden. Salt Spring was once the premier fruit producer for the province of BC, and productive old orchards still abound. Particularly worth looking for and trying are some of the heritage apples (Kings, Gravensteins, and Cox's Orange Pippins). Unlike the blandly perfect specimens in most supermarkets, these apples are usually short on eye appeal, but bear a sharply defined taste, perfume, and crunch. Drive down virtually any country road on the island to find roadside stands offering fresh eggs for sale. In late summer and throughout the fall, you will also find many stands offering a variety of vegetables and tree fruits—usually plums, apples, and pears.

Fraser's Thimble Farms (175 Arbutus Road, 250/537-5788), on the north end of the island, is a nursery of interest to gardeners, particularly those curious about indigenous species.

Local BC wines were once, deservedly, considered undrinkable plonk, but in recent years Okanagan Valley vintners have gained accolades for their white wines, especially the dessert varieties. There's also a good selection of local microbrewery beers and sweet hard ciders in Salt Spring pubs.

Dares to Be Different Cafe and Store (112 Hereford Lane) has an Organic Farmers Market every Tuesday in the parking lot. All the food offered here, in both the store and cafe, is from certified organic farms—no bovine growth hormones in the milk, no pesticide residues, no chlorine in the water served at your table. They work with organic smallholders from all over BC. Even the beer, brewed on Salt Spring at Gulf Islands Brewery, is organic. Look here for Salt Spring Seed's garlic book—an ode to the stinking rose—with 52 varieties of garlic described and available to growers ($6). Our favorite recipe in the book: Nettle Pesto made with six cups of stinging nettle leaves and garlic, and a suggestion for a bath in which you steep in garlic cloves. If you can't find the book, write to Salt Spring Seeds, PO Box 444, Ganges, BC V8K 2W1, or call 250/537-5269.

Mobile Market (see Picnics) carries Salt Spring Island Cheese Company's goat cheese—very prettily served with a pressed viola or herb leaves on top.

Kayaking. Salt Spring offers almost unlimited kayaking possibilities, and paddling among the inlets and islets will bring you nose to nose with some of the most magnificent landscapes and wildlife in the world. Circumnavigating the island takes about four days. You can camp at Cape Kepple at the south end, but watch the tides—high tide can wash out your presumably dry campsite. Burgoyne Bay is another lovely spot. At the north end, Idle Island, which is public land, offers room for three or four tents.

Day trips include paddling out to the Chain Islets (Goat, Deadman, First, Second, and Third Sisters) in Ganges Harbour. From the foot of Quebec Drive (off Long Harbour Road) beginners can paddle out to Long Harbour in a relaxed four- or five-hour trip, including time for lunch. For the more experienced and energetic, try the trip from Southey Point to Blackberry Point on Valdes Island. Nautical charts are available at any marine supply shop, or at Volume Two Bookstore, 250/537-9223, in Mouat's Mall.

Note: One of the joys of paddling is the opportunity to observe marine life. Please, however, respect the privilege. Avoid disturbing the seals, particularly in the spring when they're giving birth and raising their pups. Also, many of the islets are nesting places for birds—use binoculars to observe them, but don't try to approach. If you plan to camp overnight, please practice no-trace camping. And do remember that summer is drought season—a small campfire can easily turn into a major disaster.

Boat Rentals. Salt Spring Kayaking (250/537-4664 or 250/653-4222) rents kayaks from either Ganges or Fulford. The beginner can learn basic paddling skills in three hours of in-the-water instruction, with equipment provided. There are a number of tours, ranging from a sunset paddle around either Fulford or Ganges Harbour to several multiday trips, including a women-only sojourn. Reserve early—two months in advance for any of the summer expeditions is recommended. Salt Spring Marine Rentals (120 Upper Ganges Road, 250/537-9100) also rents kayaks, canoes, and paddleboats.

Diving. The confluence of cold, deep ocean currents and warm surface runoff from the Fraser River on the mainland results in a nutrient-rich stew that swirls in the waters surrounding the Gulf Islands. The food chain starts with plankton and works its way up to seals and whales. Underwater visibility ranges from a few feet in summer, to a few yards in winter. For color intensity and density of life among the invertebrates, the top 30 feet offers divers the best opportunities. Oxygen for air tanks and equipment are available at Moby's Marina (at Salt Spring Marina, 120 Upper Ganges Road, 250/537-9100). If nobody is around, check in the pub or on the dock.

Among the most highly recommended dives is off Arbutus Island, between Fulford and Swartz Bay. You can circumnavigate the island on a single tank of air. The shallow southeast side has the largest variety of sea life, but the steep west side offers bigger fish. The dive off Beaver Point is good, but the tides are very strong here—dive on slack tide. Forest Island offers an excellent dive for beginners, while the Pellow Islets (off Portland Island) have a sunken wreck, marked by a buoy, to explore.

Bird-watching. Unfortunately, most of the best vantage points for bird-watching are on private property, but both Ruckle Provincial Park and the Fulford estuary offer a wealth of species. California quail are plentiful on the island, and pheasants, though rarer, occasionally cause minor traffic stalls on Beaver Point Road. The sharp-eyed birder might spot juncos,

There are many marine parks among the Gulf Islands, but currents can be strong, and the water is always cold. A dry suit or a substantial wet suit is necessary. Diving is only as safe as you make it—consult current tide tables and local charts, and always dive with a buddy.

The east side of Fulford Harbour is a great spot for bird-watchers, who can expect to see herons, kingfishers, glaucous-winged gulls, American wigeons, harlequin ducks, and mute swans.

towhees, Steller's jays, Bewick's wrens, and winter wrens, as well as all three species of woodpeckers. The island's bookstores carry a good selection of field guides. There's also a birder's checklist available at Fraser's Thimble Farms (175 Arbutus Road, 250/537-5788) and at Volume Two Bookstore (at Mouat's Mall, 250/537-9223).

Golf. The Salt Spring Island Golf and Country Club (Lower Ganges Road, 250/537-2121) has a challenging nine-hole, par-72 course, open year-round. The Pro Shop is open every day, year-round. Greens fees run about $20 to $30, depending on time and day.

Blackburn Meadows (1070 Fulford-Ganges Road, 250/537-1707), Salt Spring's second public golf course, is a nine-hole, executive, par-32 course. Fees are roughly $10 to $20. There is a small clubhouse and pro shop, open March 1 to October 31. Club and pull-cart rentals are available.

Day Spas. After all this kayaking, fishing, hiking, and sun worshipping, we couldn't decide whether to soak in the Goddess Milk Bath (it seemed appropriate) or the Moor Mud Bath at Skin Sensations by the Sea (and it is, on the Ganges waterfront, 250/ 537-8807). We eventually tossed in the towel and had a Vichy water, steam, and aromatherapy treatment in a contraption that sprayed and washed while we just laid there, limp, on the table, followed by a sports pedicure (no nail polish). You can get facials, various kinds of massage with herbal oils, pedicures, manicures—the works.

Salty Springs Sea Spa Resort, 250/537-4111, on the island's north end, offers massages, facials, pedicures, and hot soaks in the very waters that give Salt Spring Island its name—you can get your astrological chart read, take a yoga class, and stay in luxury cabins overnight (see Lodgings).

RESTAURANTS

HOUSE PICCOLO ☆☆

Some of the best food in Ganges can be had at this cozy house/restaurant right in the middle of things. The menu is European with a decidedly Scandinavian slant—Swedish meatballs and Wiener schnitzel at lunch, seafood and other specialties for dinner. Try the pan-roasted breast of duckling with rosemary and cherry jus, or the roast venison with juniper and mountain-ash berries. Do not miss dessert, especially the traditional Finnish preparation of frozen cranberries with caramel sauce. *108 Hereford Ave (heading north, it's at second main intersection in town, near Thrifty Foods), Salt Spring Island, BC V8K 2V9; 250/537-1844; $$; full bar; AE, MC, V; local checks only; dinner every day.*

Salt Spring's liquor store is at Grace Point Square, around the corner from Mouat's Mall in Ganges; 250/537-5441.

MOBY'S MARINE PUB

 There are pubs, and there are great pubs. Moby's falls into the latter category, with the tastiest, most imaginative pub menu on the islands. (Psst...don't miss the baked tomato soup or the lamb burger.) Expect lots of local color, with natives and visitors jostling for elbow room in this marina-side home-away-from-home. The rotating art exhibits and great views of Ganges Harbour are almost incidental to the lively atmosphere. All this, and live music, too. *120 Upper Ganges Rd, Salt Spring Island, BC V8K 2V9; 250/537-5559; $; full bar; MC, V; no checks; lunch, dinner everyday.*

"We go to the movies, have dinner with friends, go out to Moby's on jazz nights—in general, we do pretty much what we did in the city for fun, just not as much of it."
—Paul Eastman, B&B host

VESUVIUS INN

 The big draws at this rebuilt version of a turn-of-the-century loggers' and fishermen's inn are the variety of brews and the spectacular view from the waterside porch of the ferry dock, with Crofton in the distance. This is a very casual place—order a Caesar salad or some fish 'n' chips at the bar as you go in, and find a good spot on the porch. *805 Vesuvius Bay Rd (at the northwest point of the island), Salt Spring Island, BC V8K 1L6; 250/537-2312; $; full bar; MC, V; no checks; open 11am-11pm every day.*

LODGINGS

THE BEACH HOUSE ON SUNSET DRIVE

 This extraordinary property a few kilometers north of Vesuvius is in a league of its own. Jon De West, an affable, gregarious expatriate from the Vancouver rat race, and his wife, Maureen, a former instructor from the Cordon Bleu, were born to be B&B hosts. Coffee is delivered to each room in the morning, and Maureen's four-course breakfasts, served around the big table in the view dining room, are legendary. The sprawling home lies right on the ocean, enjoying warm currents sweeping up from the south that heat the surf to bathtub temperature in spring and summer. Three large guest rooms (all have their own private entrance), one with a cathedral ceiling, fireplace, and double bathroom with claw-foot tub and marble shower (outside on the deck is a warm shower), are all in a private wing of the main house. Linens and towels are top of the line at this inn, and all rooms are furnished with baskets filled with extra touches. But the best is the namesake Beach Cottage, a cozy refurbished boathouse with a wraparound deck, kitchenette, bedroom, and breathtaking sunset vista. This one has honeymoon written all over it. *930 Sunset Dr (up Sunset Dr from Vesuvius Bay, RR 1), Salt Spring Island, BC V8K 1E6; 250/ 537-2879; beachhouse@saltspring.com; www.saltspring.com/ beachhouse; $$$; MC, V; checks OK.*

BEDDIS HOUSE BED AND BREAKFAST ☆

 With all the bed-and-breakfasts on Salt Spring, it should be easy to find one on the water, but it isn't. That makes Beddis House special, since the charming white shingled-and-clapboard farmhouse (built in 1900) and the next-door coach house (modern, but in harmonizing style) are close to a private beach on Ganges Harbour, hidden away at the end of a country road, far enough from town that you can see the stars at night and the seals and otters in the daytime. The coach house contains three very private rooms with claw-foot tubs, country-style furniture, woodstoves, and decks or balconies that look out toward the water. Breakfast and afternoon tea are served in the old house, where you will also find a guest lounge. *131 Miles Ave (follow Beddis Rd from Fulford-Ganges Rd, turn left onto Miles Rd), Salt Spring Island, BC V8K 2E1; 250/537-1028; beddis@saltspring.com; www. saltspring.com/beddishouse; $$$; MC, V; no checks.*

BOLD BLUFF RETREAT ★★

 Accessible only by boat (Tamar Griggs picks you up at Burgoyne Bay), Bold Bluff Retreat is the perfect antidote to even the most stress-filled day: 100 acres of rock, trees, and moss, including a mile of waterfront with eagles, seals, and serenity for company. The Garden Cottage, behind the main house on a cove facing Samsun Narrows and Vancouver Island, has two bedrooms, a claw-foot tub, a kitchen, a big dining and living area, duvets, and a woodstove. Salty's Cabin, available from April through October, is a five-minute walk through the forest, completely private on an even tinier cove, where the tide rushes in under the deck and the cabin. You can swim here in August; clamber along the rocks and investigate the tide pools the rest of the year. There's no power at the cabin: instead, you'll find a woodstove, a propane cooking stove and fridge, a composting toilet, and an outdoor hot-water shower under the trees. Climb up the bluff and sit on a level with the eagles, looking out over the narrows to see the tide surge through. Explore the shoreline if you have a canoe or kayak. Bring your own food, and settle in for a stay completely removed from anywhere. Three-night minimum stay summers. *Bold Bluff (accessible by boat from Burgoyne Bay), Salt Spring Island, BC V8K 2A6; 250/653-43771; boldbluff@saltspring.com; www.salt-spring. bc.ca/boldbluff; $$$; no credit cards; checks OK.*

"*The unique thing about Salt Spring is its juxtaposition of sea and landscape. There are three distinct habitats—the ocean that surrounds us; the Mediterranean, parklike setting in the south; and the arctic moss forests in the north.*"
—**Robert Bateman, artist**

HASTINGS HOUSE ★★★★

 Standing in all its gentrified splendor and imbued with an almost formidable air of genteel hospitality, Hastings House aspires to being the ultimate country retreat. It very nearly achieves that goal. The setting is postcard-perfect, the accommodations both luxurious and distinctive, and, under the watchful eye of manager Mark Gottaas, the service impeccable. It's also less snooty than it used to be under the previous owners: visitors report less of a sense that they have to live up to their surroundings, although they still have to fork out a significant amount of dough for accommodations—about $500 a night. Four restored farm buildings and a cottage, surrounded by meadows, gardens, gnarled fruit trees, and rolling lawns, overlook a peaceful cove. The 17 suites are all beautifully furnished, each with gas fireplace or wood-burning stove, wet bar, sitting area, and touches such as down comforters and artwork. Seven new suites are on the hillside above the manor house with views over the harbor, all with king beds, gas fireplaces, and decks. We like the Post—a charming garden cottage with antique wicker furniture. In the reconstructed barn, we prefer the Hayloft, with its bay window seat, Franklin stove, and quaint folk art. Perfect for two couples is the two-story, two-suite, stucco-and-half-timbered Farmhouse. In the Tudor-style Manor House, the two upstairs rooms have prime water views through leaded casement windows; the only drawback is that the kitchen and dining room are directly below. Included in the stiff tariff—this is the most expensive place in the Gulf Islands—are wake-up coffee and muffins delivered to your room, a delectable breakfast, and afternoon tea seated around the huge stone hearth in the Manor House. No children under 16.

Whether you stay at Hastings House or not, you should reserve a place at Marcel Kauer's table d'hôte dinner. Traditionally served in the handsome Tudor dining room, it is now also available in a less formal dining area (gentlemen, jacket and tie not required) and at a table for two right in the kitchen, where fascinated diners can watch food preparation—all part of the attempt to make Hastings House a little less stuffy. Dinner begins with cocktails on the lawn or in the parlor, and progresses through five expertly prepared and beautifully presented courses, all served by a knowledgeable and gracious staff. An appetizer might be junipered venison carpaccio with asparagus and sunflower oil, followed by a carrot and orange bisque, then marinated grilled sea bass with spinach and a tomato *coulis*. You have five choices of entrée: usually a Salt Spring lamb dish, perhaps Fraser Valley duck breast with braised onions and cranberries; other entrées are dependent on the season and the mood of chef Kauer. The ingredients are local, and the fruit, vegetables, and herbs are often from the inn's own gardens. *160 Upper Ganges Rd (just north of Ganges), Salt Spring Island, BC V8K 2S2; 250/537-2362; hastingshouse@*

saltspring.com; www.hastingshouse.com; $$$; full bar; AE, MC, V; local checks only; dinner daily.

THE OLD FARMHOUSE ☆☆☆

On this island boasting nearly a hundred bed-and-breakfasts, the Old Farmhouse stands out. German-born hosts Gertie and Karl Fuss have turned their heritage farmhouse into an inn worthy of *House Beautiful*. Four guest rooms, each with a private bath and a patio or balcony, are charmingly decorated: brilliant whitewashed wainscoting, crisp floral wallpaper, stained-glass and leaded windows, French doors, polished pine floors, feather beds and starched duvets, a bouquet of fresh roses. It's all here, and scrupulously maintained by very professional hosts (who know everything about the island, down to all the ferry times). A gazebo, a hammock, and a couple of porch swings abet the appearance and reality of near-perfect relaxation. Morning coffee is delivered to your room, followed by an elegant and copious breakfast at the country dining room table. There's not a detail these hosts miss: they even supply doggie bags (so you can take the inevitable extras with you for an afternoon picnic), then suggest the best picnic spot. *1077 North End Rd (4 km/2½ miles north of Ganges), Salt Spring Island, BC V8K 1L9; 250/537-4113; $$; MC, V; checks OK.*

A PERFECT PERCH ☆

 Short of the top of Mount Maxwell, this place has one of the best views you'll find on Salt Spring: 1,000 feet above the sea, looking out over the Gulf Islands and the Strait of Georgia, taking in the Canadian and American mainland mountains. This is almost sybaritic comfort: recline in the double Roman soaker tub in the Parker Suite while you watch the flames dance in the double-sided fireplace, and look through the wide glass windows to the misty straits far below. The old-fashioned wedding dress on the wall above the four-poster bed leaves no doubt that this suite is intended for honeymooners. All three rooms are comfortable and luxurious. Host Libby Jutras sometimes presents Mexican dishes for breakfast (don't worry, she'll ask first); if you're lucky, her commercial-fisherman husband will

"Small is beautiful. What's nice to do with a small group of friends is not necessarily nice when the whole world wants to do it, too."

—Robert Bateman, naturalist, artist

have brought something home from the sea. *225 Armand Way (Fulford-Ganges Rd to Dukes Rd, up the hill to Seymour Heights, then onto Armand Way—don't give up), Salt Spring Island, BC V8K 2B6; 888/663-2030 or 250/653-2030; ljutras@saltspring.com; www.saltspring.com/perfectperch; $$$; MC, V; checks OK; (closed Dec–Feb).*

SPINDRIFT

 Spindrift is that most precious of commodities in island resorts: a place on the ocean, private, secluded, quiet, with forest walks outside your door. The six oceanfront cottages on 6 acres of the Welbury Point Peninsula all have ocean views, wood-burning fireplaces, and full kitchens. Each is named for a woman who fought for women's rights. We like Charlotte, with its oceanfront deck, and Henrietta's Rose— the most private and spacious of the cottages—but others prefer the studio duplexes Amelia and Rose, for their decks on both ocean and land sides, for daylong sunshine. Here you'll find no telephones, no televisions (except in Rose); just the long private stroll around the peninsula, the quiet coves ideal for watching seals and eagles, the deer and rabbits that poke curious noses toward you, and the resident dog menagerie. Adults only; quiet leashed pets are allowed by prior arrangement. *255 Welbury Pt Dr (on Welbury Point, near Long Harbour ferry terminal), Salt Spring Island, BC V8K 2L7; 250/537-5311; www.salt-spring.bc.ca/sprindrift/; $$–$$$; no credit cards; checks OK.*

WESTON LAKE INN

The owners of this contemporary farmhouse just above Weston Lake—Susan Evans, Ted Harrison, and Cass (their sheepdog)—have become experts at fading into the background and letting their guests enjoy the comfortable space. Their touches are everywhere: in Harrison's petit-point embroideries, framed and hanging in the three guest rooms; in Evans's excellent, hearty breakfasts (with vegetables from their organic garden); and in the blooming results of their gardening efforts. Paintings by local artists, including Evans's mother, hang on the walls. Outside are lovingly developed ornamental and produce gardens for guests to walk through or sit in. The couple tries to grow as much of the produce they use as possible, and breakfast can include homemade jams, home-laid eggs, herbs, asparagus, berries, and—in a good year—their own apple juice. Evans knows and loves her island and is a fount of local knowledge. Guests have access to two living rooms, one a comfortable lounge with fireplace, library, TV, and VCR (including a decent collection of videos), and to the hot tub out on the deck. Ted offers charters aboard the 36-foot sailing sloop *Malaika*. This inn is a great island value. *813 Beaver Point Rd (3½ km/2⅕ miles east of Fulford Harbour ferry dock), Salt Spring Island, BC V8K 1X9; 250/653-4311; stay@westonlakeinn.com; www.westonlakeinn.com; $$; MC, V; checks OK.*

NORTH AND SOUTH PENDER ISLANDS

Pender Island is actually two islands—North and South Pender—which are separated by a turn-of-the-century man-made canal and joined by a rackety wooden bridge. These are among the quietest and most self-protective islands in the whole southern Gulf Islands archipelago. Not coincidentally, North Pender is also the only island with a major suburban-style residential development—Magic Lake Estates, an architectural faux pas that mobilized Pender Islanders (and, eventually, neighboring islanders) to protect their environments from similar rampant destruction. While there are no statistics on this, the Penders seem to have a higher concentration of retirees and part-time residents than any of the other islands, with the possible exception of Mayne. The locals are not particularly unfriendly, but they are self-contained. The local economy doesn't depend on tourism. There are a few waterfront restaurants, a historic grocery store that has been converted into an art gallery, artists' studios, and a nicely landscaped one-stop shopping center, with groceries, butcher, baker, and liquor.

These days, the Penders (Magic Lake Estates excepted) retain their bucolic charm. The topography is relatively gentle, particularly around the more heavily populated North Pender. The many farms and old frame houses that dot this part of the island tend to be trim and well kept, with bountiful gardens. South Pender is all rocky cliff and tree-covered mountain (Beaumont Marine Provincial Park), with a twisty road snaking around it on the east side.

"We like just about everything about Pender, but we particularly appreciate the closeness to nature, the variety of landscapes, and the wonderful range of people here."

—David Spalding, author and naturalist

ACTIVITIES

Sight-seeing. For an overview of both North and South Pender, take Otter Bay Road to the top of the hill, then turn onto Bedwell Harbour Road. This becomes Canal Road, which takes you across the canal to South Pender. Canal Road leads eventually to Spalding Road, and here you can turn left and follow Green Burn Lake out to Gowland Point, or turn right and explore Boundary Pass. Retrace your route to get back to North Pender.

GETTING AROUND

The Pender Island ferry terminal is at Otter Bay, on the northwest end of North Pender. Several ferries make the trip daily to and from Tsawwassen (on the mainland), also servicing the other southern Gulf Islands. Coming from the mainland, Pender is the second-to-last stop. There are also daily sailings from Otter Bay to Swartz Bay on Vancouver Island. On Pender Island, you can rent a nice car from Vivian Mitchell's Local Motion Car Rentals, 250/629-3366, for about $30 a day (and she'll deliver it). You can also hitch a ride with Pender Island Taxi, 250/629-9900.

Another tour takes you from the ferry terminal at Otter Bay up the steep hill to Port Washington Road. Follow it either left to Port Washington, a little community of a few old island homes gathered around Grimmer Bay, or head right to Hope Bay, a similarly charming cluster, with signs to artists' studios along the way.

Otter Bay Marina is built on the site where a Japanese settler once owned a saltworks. Hyashi Cove is named after him.

Island History. Old photographs of the Penders' first settlers and of the dredging of the canal between the two islands are displayed at the island's library on North Pender. This display, put together by the Pender Island Museum Society, includes artifacts found in the shell midden near the canal. The library is next to North Pender's old school, built in 1902, in use until 1977.

Shopping. More interesting than the Driftwood Shopping Centre is the cluster of shops at Hope Bay Village, relocated after the historic Hope Bay Store burned in 1998. The Goldsmith Shop, 250/629-9990, specializing in jewelry restoration and repair, is in its same location "in the little shack up on the hill," above the old wharf where the store once stood, but The Galloping Moon Gallery (1325 McKinnon Rd, 250/629-6020) relocated after the fire and has re-created the Hope Bay Store inventory with a broad selection of arts, crafts, and espresso drinks. The Port Washington Store, another old general store (built in 1910), with lovely wood floors and clapboard siding on North Pender's north end, has been turned into a browser's store of local arts and crafts and coffees as well.

Arts and Crafts. The Armstrong Gallery (1201 Otter Bay Road, 250/629-6571) at Port Washington has a fine collection of maritime and wildlife art in a variety of media. Renaissance Studios, 250/629-3070, is one of those anomalies of island life; Jan and Milada Huk's shop reflects their interests: glass beads, hundreds of them strung into necklaces and other jewelry; art and antique restoration; and woven rugs—one of the most interesting browser's stores in the islands. Potters Roger and Harriet Stribley bought one of the island's oldest houses, refurbished it, and built a potters studio, Pender Island Pottery, 250/629-6662, on the property above Hope Bay. Look for the (real) teapot perched on top of the sign. Master horologist Wilf Craven runs the Clock Shop (2234 Port Washington Road, 250/629-3253; by appointment only) from his heritage home, where he buys, sells, and repairs antique watches and clocks. Most Pender studios are open only on weekends. Call ahead.

Pender Islanders have been particularly adept at saving their foreshore for themselves. As a bonus for the visitor, this translates into more beaches, and easier beach access, than on any of the other islands.

Farm and Garden. On Saturdays from late spring through fall, there's a farmers market on the perimeter of the Driftwood Shopping Centre, at the junction of Bedwell Harbour Road and Razor Point Road. Though smaller and less colorful than Salt Spring's market, this is a good place to pick up organic fruits and vegetables, homemade preserves, fresh flowers and herbs, and crafts. You'll also find produce at roadside stands around the island, and a great little organic grocery (the inventory here is truly remarkable) on North Pender.

Joyful Symmetry Country Cottage & Garden (3309 Port Washington Road, 250/629-6476) carries dried flower and herbal arrangements, as well as an imaginative assortment of twig furniture and smaller craft variations on a theme of gardens and orchards.

For health-oriented groceries, visit Southridge Farms Country Store, 250/629-2051, on Port Washington Road. You can pick up tofu, vitamins, fresh veggies, and free-range eggs, as well as Haggis Farm organic breads. The outside of the building looks unremarkable, inside is filled with a remarkable array of both organic and unusual specialty food items.

Old Orchard Farm, one of Pender's oldest farms (1891) has eggs, flowers, and fruit for sale in their little roadside stand outside the gate on Port Washington Road.

Hiking. There are several well-marked trails on the Penders, most of which go through the three provincial parks—Prior Centennial Provincial Park on North Pender, and Mount Norman and Beaumont Marine Provincial Parks (which lie back to back) on South Pender. The hike up Mount Norman is particularly recommended. It can be climbed from the road, an easy walk compared to the hike from the shoreline, in about 30 minutes or less to a wooden platform overlooking the bays and inlets between the Gulf Islands and Vancouver Island, particularly at sunset. The main trailhead for this climb is off Ainslie Point Road, a right turn after the bridge across the canal. Watch for signs.

Snacks. For a very decent and generously portioned burger or other quick snacks to go, the Stand (at Otter Bay terminal, 250/629-3292) is perhaps the best value-for-food-dollar on the island. Libby's Village Bakery (at the Driftwood Shopping Centre, 250/629-6453) is a good spot for a quick lunch of soup, sandwich, and fresh pastry.

Beach Walking. Perhaps the best thing about the Penders is public access to beaches. At last count, there were nearly 30 public accesses to waterfront, covering the gamut of possibilities from small and semiprivate to expansive and wildly popular. Mortimer Spit, on South Pender immediately opposite the bridge between the islands, is one of the nicest. Sandy and strewn with driftwood, it's easy to get to, but feels isolated and wild. Gowland Point Beach, at the extreme south end of South Pender, is similarly easy to reach and a great spot for that feeling of splendid solitude. At Brooks Point, at the end of Gowland Point Road, are 10 acres of coastal headlands secured for the public by the Pender Conservancy Association. Too close to a popular pub and marina, but still worth a visit, is Medicine Beach on Bedwell Harbour, with waterfront, marsh, and 20 acres of upland forest with a registered archaeological site (shell midden). Hike over the top of Mount Norman from Ainslie Point Road (see Hiking), then take the turnoff to Beaumont Marine Provincial Park. The trail to the marine park is about 30 minutes downhill to the west side of South Pender, where you'll have Beaumont Marine Park's splendid rocks and little crescent beaches nearly to yourself. Watch for signs or pick up a map to sites from Windemere

Real Estate in the Driftwood Shopping Centre or at the Info Centre near the ferry landing at Otter Bay.

Cycling. The Penders are particularly friendly to two-wheelers. The terrain is gentler and more bicycle-friendly than on the other Gulf Islands, though the roads are not necessarily in better shape. Except for the inevitable crush of summer motorists, the roads are quiet and traffic-free. You can rent mountain bikes at Otter Bay Marina (2311 McKinnon Road, 250/629-3579), but you need to reserve ahead.

Camping. Prior Centennial Provincial Park on North Pender has 17 campsites in the forest above Port Browning. For those who like to camp but don't want to cook, the campground is convenient to a pub. Sites can be reserved (see Camping in the Gulf Islands).

Beaumont Marine Provincial Park on South Pender has 11 tent sites in a lovely forest setting next to the beach. This truly is a beautiful campground; access is from the water or by hiking over the hill from Mount Norman. Unfortunately, there's no public parking overnight up on Mount Norman, so you'll have to be inventive. You could kayak from Bedwell Harbour Marina, but again, parking is a problem. It is worth the trouble to figure it out.

Marinas. Boaters will find moorage and supplies at several places in the Penders. On the northwest side of North Pender, Otter Bay Marina, 250/629-3579, has overnight moorage with power and water hookups, laundry, showers, and groceries, as well as protection from the ferry wash from the nearby terminal. Bedwell Harbour Island Resort & Marina, 800/663-2899 or 250/629-3212, on South Pender has a resort hotel, marina, store, post office, and fuel, as well as the Canada Customs office for U.S. boaters during the summer months and a terrific pub overlooking the harbor. In nearby Bedwell Harbour, you'll find mooring docks and buoys, good anchorage, walking trails, hand-pumped water, camping and picnicking facilities, and washrooms.

Port Browning Marina, 250/629-3493, is in a pretty setting at the head of the small bay between North and South Pender. It has a well-used look, but people are friendly, the beer is good, the cafe serves up a tasty cheap breakfast, there's camping in the old orchard, there's a swimming pool, and it's a ½-mile walk to the

Mouat Point Kayaks on Otter Bay (at Otter Bay Marina on North Pender, 250/629-6767) rents kayaks during the summer season.

"Solo canoeing around the islands is not an easy thing to do, because of the winds. Kayaking allows you to get into all the little bays and estuaries around the island."
—Robert Bateman, naturalist, artist

The island's only
bank is at the com-
mercial center of
the island, the
Driftwood Shopping
Centre, at the junc-
tion of Bedwell
Harbour Road and
Razor Point Road.

Driftwood Shopping Centre. There are government docks (pub-lic wharfs) at Port Washington, Port Browning, and Hope Bay.

 Golf. Pender Island Golf & Country Club is a charming and challenging nine-hole course, with licensed club-house, pro shop, and clubs and cart rentals. Par 66 for men, 69 for women. Greens fees are $20 for nine holes, $30 for 18. (2305 Otter Bay Road, 250/629-6659, or write Box 6, Pender Island, BC V0N 2M0.)

LODGINGS

BEDWELL HARBOUR ISLAND RESORT

This sprawling, family-owned resort complex, in operation for decades and still feeling very much like the early 1960s, includes a marina, rooms, cabins, villas in a condo building, a pub, and a restaurant. This is all going to change, however, as the resort undergoes extensive renovations that began in October 1999 and will continue over the next few years. Con-dos will stay, but cabins, hotel, and commercial buildings will be torn down and replaced. The resort is in an ideal South Pender location: a perfectly sheltered cove and marina at the foot of dramatic rock cliffs, backed by a gentle, wooded hillside, with stunning sunset views. The rooms and cabins (long a part of the resort) have woodstoves, balconies or decks, kitchens or kitchenettes, and sweeping views. Call or check the web site to see if they are still standing. Newer, more luxurious accommodations are available in the condo-miniums—two-bedroom villas done in pine, with fully equipped kitchens, fireplaces, and decks. Restaurant and pub are also slated for demolition, we're sorry to say, because the pub is perfectly charming as is. Restaurant chef Nora Bru-lotte, who has been with the resort for years, loves to experi-ment, and her menus change from year to year. The waterfront pub offers typical pub fare—and a great view. *9801 Spalding Rd (follow Canal Rd from the bridge to Spalding, then to Bedwell Harbour), South Pender Island, BC V0N 2M3; 250/629-3212 or 800/663-2899; bedwell@islandnet.com; www.islandnet.com/bedwell/; $$; full bar; AE, MC, V; no checks; breakfast, lunch (in pub), dinner every day (closed Oct–Mar).*

OCEANSIDE INN

 Geoff Clydesdale, for years the owner of a Vancouver travel agency, bought the old Cliffside Inn several years ago, and has completely refurbished it into a proper country inn. Of course, this particular country inn is perched on a cliff overlooking the channel, islands, and stunning views of Mount Baker, with stairs to a mile-long beach (rare in the islands), and it is wonderfully private. Each of the four bright and cheery bedrooms has a private entrance and its own hot tub on a private deck. Three rooms face the ocean; the fourth faces the garden. Both the Garden Suite and Channel View Suite (lots of glass, with its own sitting room) have fireplaces. The kitchen was the first thing Geoff replaced, and out of it are borne such delicacies as marinated grilled salmon served with lemon lime dill sauce and full breakfasts that include fresh salmon omelettes, blackberry pancakes, and the like. We have not rated this at press time as the inn is still undergoing renovation. *4230 Armadale Rd (follow signs to Hope Bay, turn on Clam Bay Rd to Armadale), North Pender Island, BC V0N 2M0; 250/629-6691; www.penderisland.com; $$; V; no checks.*

The **Pender Post,** **published monthly, is a hybrid publication that is part newsletter, part magazine, and part services directory. At $2.50, it's a bargain for the events calendar alone. Pick up a copy at the Driftwood Shopping Centre.**

MAYNE ISLAND

Today, tiny Mayne Island is shy and retiring, though this wasn't always the case. Those who spend some time at the Plumper Pass Lock-Up (the island's museum) will discover there's actually a robust and rakish history behind the bucolic facade of this gently rustic landscape.

Mayne is not an island for shopping addicts. Artists' studios, including a glass foundry, are open to the public for only a limited number of hours, and mostly in the summer. This smallest of the southern Gulf Islands can reveal itself to bicyclers (but beware of narrow roads, blind curves, and hills) and drivers alike in the course of a single day, but it's enchanting enough to justify a much longer stay.

Mayne has some of the nicest beaches in all of the southern islands. Public access is at Bennett Bay, Campbell Bay, Oyster Bay, Piggot Bay, and Dinner Bay Park.

ACTIVITIES

Island History. In its formative years, Mayne was known as "Little Hell," because of the number of pubs that dotted the island. This reputation, and the enterprises that supported it, was fostered, no doubt, by the numbers of miners who made Mayne—precisely halfway between Victoria and the mouth of the Fraser River—a regular stop on their way to the Fraser gold-fields during the rush of 1858. In these less rowdy times, the current tourist brochure recommends gin and tonic as a refreshing antidote to the annual summertime drought. Not mentioned is that Coast Salish peoples used these same routes and stopping points through the islands on their way to the Fraser River from as far south as the Olympia area in southern Puget Sound.

The picturesque lighthouse and Coast Guard station at Active Pass on Georgina Point Road is, reportedly, the only place in the Gulf Islands where Capt. George Vancouver actually landed when he explored the coastline in 1792. You can tour the lighthouse and the grounds at Georgina Point Heritage Park between 1 and 3pm. On nearby Campbell Bay (via Waugh Road), there's a public beach with good beachcombing potential.

Start at Village Bay Road and wind your way around Miner's Bay, locale for the island's picturesque old village, to Fernhill, the main route across the island. Just past the health center and school on your left, you can swing down Fernhill to Bennett Bay,

There are no commercial marinas on Mayne, but there are two very busy government docks—one at Horton Bay, and the other at Miner's Bay. Pleasure boaters can anchor out, or consider docking at nearby Galiano Island and rowing over to Mayne.

GETTING THERE

Of all the southern Gulf Islands, Mayne is reportedly the one that is easiest to get to (and get off), but it depends on whom you talk with. Residents complain of overloads, odd days, and often changing ferry schedules.

There are two ferries daily between Salt Spring and Mayne, and between Mayne and Tsawwassen; four between Mayne and Pender or Galiano and Swartz Bay, and two to Saturna. The ferry terminal is at Village Bay.

or take a right and follow Horton Bay Road to Horton Bay. This route will take you past some of the island's oldest farms and orchards. The well-protected waters of Horton Bay are a favorite anchorage for a community of nomadic houseboaters who tow their homes from cove to cove among the Gulf Islands.

Arts and Crafts. Painters, candlemakers, glass blowers, jewelers, potters—they're all here. Pick up a directory to Mayne Island from any Info Centre in the Gulf Islands for a current list of studios. Last count was about 13. Look here for painters Jim McKenzie and Frances Faminow, framers (handmade, exquisite frames by Beverley Shewfelt and Anthony Mitchell), and potters John Carowsky and Jeanne Lewis. There are several small shops selling Persian rugs and home decor items, open weekends or by appointment.

Farm and Garden. Foodies of the carnivorous persuasion should make a point of heading out to the Arbutus Bay Deer Farms (777 Beachwood Drive, 250/539-2301) for organic fallow deer. Virtually cholesterol- and fat-free, this is an expensive but delicious treat. Available as roasts, chops, steaks, and sausages, or in packaged, preservative-free stews and pâtés.

Picnics. You can pick up breads, pastries, and espresso from Manna Bakery Café, 250/539-2323, and groceries from two stores: Miners Bay Trading Post near the Government Wharf in Active Pass and Tru Value Foods (they have bulk items, such as trail mix) in the Maynestreet Mall, also near the Government Wharf.

Chef Steve Cruise, formerly with Sooke Harbor House, has his own little Miners Bay Cafe, open for breakfast and lunch with homemade bread, soups, and vegetarian dishes; 250/539-9888. You might want to tuck an extra lunch into a bag and eat it for dinner on the beach.

Mayne Island Kayak and Canoe, 250/539-2667, rents kayaks and canoes from $17 for two hours, and will arrange complimentary ferry pickups and drop-offs.

Hiking. Mayne has no public hiking trails, but the slow pace of life and the lack of heavy traffic make its country roads a more-than-pleasant amble. There's a great little walk through the Indian Reserve out to Helen Point, about 1 kilometer west of Village Bay. Look for the power lines, or ask a local to point out the trail for you. The path winds through a mossy forest and ends up at a grassy promontory from which you can watch seals, eagles, and sea lions feeding on the rich smorgasbord of sea life that inhabits Active Pass, the narrow passageway between Mayne and Galiano Islands.

Mount Parke is a major new provincial park, with parking areas and marked trails to the summit. Follow signs for parking and trailheads. The vistas over Active Pass are spectacular, and the mosses underfoot are home to an intricate carpet of more than 250 varieties of wildflowers. Resist the urge to pick yourself a bouquet.

Bird-watching. Bald eagles, terns, and seagulls are regular sights on any of the Gulf Islands. Mayne seems to have a particular abundance of smaller species. In spring, you'll spot hummingbirds and swallows. Summer brings goldfinches and cedar waxwings. In autumn, migrating flocks of shorebirds rest on the mudflats at Horton and Village Bays. In winter, look for buffleheads, wigeons, goldeneyes, and mallards in the bays and coves.

Camping. Mayne campgrounds include Journey's End Farm, at the end of Simpson Road on the south-central side of the island; 250/539-2411. No electrical hookups or sewer facilities ($15 a night), but there's 300 feet of waterfront on 60 acres overlooking Navy Channel. Fern Hollow, 250/539-5253, on Horton Bay Road, has about 10 sites in "Provincial campground style" in the woods.

Albatross Charters
(at Point Road,
250/539-2244) has
a 30-foot power-
boat with tackle
onboard. Rates
from $55 per hour,
no minimum. Char-
ters can be tailored
to your interests.

RESTAURANTS

SPRINGWATER LODGE

There are few options for eats on Mayne Island, but for reliable, inexpensive food you could do worse than to sink your teeth into a burger on the deck of the Springwater Lodge. Funky rusticity is the general theme of the decor here, but the setting—on the edge of a pretty, leafy little village—and the genial, low-key atmosphere make this an appealing choice. And it's open year-round for breakfast, lunch, and dinner—rare indeed. *400 Fernhill Road (from ferry, head toward Miner's Bay), Mayne Island, BC V0N 4J0; 250/539-5521; www.gulfislands.com/springwater; $; MC, V; no checks; breakfast, lunch, dinner every day.*

LODGINGS

BLUE VISTA RESORT

For something quieter than the Springwater Lodge, try the Blue Vista. Eight small cabins—some with one bedroom, some with two; some with woodstoves—surround a shaded courtyard with swings and things for little people. Cabins have kitchens (BYO groceries) and a porch—perfect for settling in with a good book. Picnic tables, barbecues, rowboats, and bicycles are provided. Across the street from Bennett Bay. Ask about off-season discounts. *563 Arbutus Road (RR 1, Box C19), Mayne Island, BC V0N 2J0; 250/539-2463; $; MC, V; checks OK.*

A COACH HOUSE ON OYSTER BAY

 When you're lounging in the hot tub a few feet from the high tide line at Heather and Brian Johnston's bed-and-breakfast, it's difficult even to remember what stress is. These relative newcomers to Mayne seem to have grasped right away what it's all about: watching the seals, otters, and eagles; strolling to the lighthouse around the corner at low tide; gazing across the Strait of Georgia at the mainland mountains. Brian, an architect by trade, has designed three fine and spacious rooms in a house that looks like a 1900 coach house (mahogany wood floors and lovely wood trims) with all the modern amenities. The Landau, upstairs, is the best, with a private deck and hot tub overlooking a good view of the sea. The Hansom and Cabriolet Rooms are downstairs; the Cabriolet has an expansive view. All rooms have four-poster beds with lambswool duvets, fireplaces, and French doors. And the common rooms are filled with original art, antiques, and even a 165-year-old grand piano that is kept tuned for guests. Breakfast is four courses, and includes fruit, cereal, fresh-baked muffins, and a hot dish such as eggs Benedict or strawberry crêpes; coffee and tea come to your door a half hour before breakfast. Certified scuba divers, the Johnstons can advise on dive sites; they'll also arrange for kayak rentals—delivered to the door—and charter boat cruises. Bicycles are available for guests. *511 Bayview Dr (call for directions), Mayne Island, BC V0N 2J0; 888/629-6322 or 250/539-3368; www.bbcanada.com/acoachhouse; $$$; MC, V; checks OK.*

Tennis courts are behind the fire hall, on Felix Jack Road, just opposite the health center and school on Fernhill. As one innkeeper says, "You won't confuse them with the center court at Wimbledon, but our [island's] tennis courts are fine for a good workout."

FERNHILL LODGE ☆

The Crumblehulme eccentric taste permeates every corner, from Mary's vast collection of English pewter to the eclectic selection of books in the library to the three guest rooms, each decorated in a period theme: Moroccan, East Indian—both with private decks and hot tubs—and Jacobean, which some might find dark and a bit severe. Guests are welcome to stroll through the herb garden or enjoy the sauna, located down a path and through the garden. Brian Crumble-hulme's passion is cooking, and he'll prepare an interesting and unusual evening feast on prior notice (dinner is set—the dining room seats up to 24—and is arranged by reservation only). The Crumblehulmes' hospitality is boundless—from loaning bikes to sharing a soothing cup of tea out on the patio. Fernhill Lodge is not on the water, but has distant water views from its perch on a hill in the middle of the island. A good swimming beach is not too far. *C4 Fernhill Rd (left onto Village Bay Rd from the ferry terminal, go about 3.5 miles to Fernhill Rd), Mayne Island, BC V0N 2J0; 250/539-2544; www.gulfislands.com/fernhilllodge; $$; MC, V; checks OK; dinner every day, brunch Sun.*

OCEANWOOD COUNTRY INN ★★★

 This fine island inn continues to garner rave reviews for its facilities, its location, its cuisine—but most of all for the hospitality of its owners, Jonathan and Marilyn Chilvers. Truly innkeepers' innkeepers, they seem as accustomed as ever to meeting the needs of their guests, thinking of everything, right down to a written list of nearby scenic walks. Oceanwood underwent major renovations in 1995, increasing the square footage (there are now 12 rooms) and moving the dining room to face the water. The best of the accommodations is the Wisteria Suite, with a soaking tub on one of two private decks overlooking Navy Channel. Rooms have some combination of fireplace, soaking tub or whirlpool tub, deck or balcony, and views of either the water or the garden—an Oceanwood feature, with herbs, spring bulbs, roses, lavender, dahlias, and other showy seasonal performers. The setting, with tree-webbed views of Navy Channel and distant islands, is lovely.

Breakfasts are innovative and hearty, with breads baked by chef Paul McKinnon and features such as homemade sausage or orange French toast with raspberry purée. At teatime, you can munch on cookies and watch the eagles, or chat with fellow guests. Fresh, local products are emphasized in their dining room: you might find steelhead on the menu, or get to taste bread baked with four kinds of wild mushrooms. Dinner is a set four-course menu, with two choices of main course. The wine list is carefully chosen, and the dining room suitably intimate. Coffee (or something off the admirable list of ports and single-malt Scotches) by the fire in the library is the perfect finale. *630 Dinner Bay Rd (right on Dalton Dr, right on Mariners, immediate left onto Dinner Bay Rd; look for sign), Mayne Island, BC V0N 2J0; 250/539-5074; oceanwood@gulfislands.com; www.oceanwood.com; $$$; full bar; MC, V; Canadian checks only; dinner every day (closed Dec–Mar).*

SPRINGWATER LODGE

 Established in 1892, the Springwater is reportedly the oldest continually operated hotel in British Columbia. And, other than sleeping under the stars (which merits consideration on warm summer nights), it's also among the cheapest island lodgings ($40). The charmingly dilapidated lodge has six bedrooms; the bathrooms are old, but for character, price, and friendly people, it's a fine spot indeed. There are two duplex cabins, each with two bedrooms, kitchen, and bath ($85). Sometimes at night, local folksingers will drop by and entertain the guests and island residents. *400 Fernhill Road (from ferry, head toward Miner's Bay), Mayne Island, BC V0N 4J0; 250/539-5521; www.gulfislands.com/springwater; $; MC, V; no checks.*

"I like the energy of the island. There's lots of it, but it's slowed down to a human pace. People have the time to do the things they really want to do." —Michael Gluss, photographer

YOU SAY MADRONA

You say madrona (or madrone or madrono), I say arbutus. But they're the same lovely, cinnamon-barked tree—belonging to a family of a dozen arbutus species worldwide, all of them part of the larger family of broad leaf evergreens that includes rhododendrons, azaleas, and mountain laurel. The tree's red bark curls back to reveal the smooth olive green limbs, the blossoms are droops of white stars, the clumps of red berries in late summer attract hundreds of birds. Ketzel Levine, National Public Radio commentator, describes Arbutus menziesii *as "sleek, burnt-orange bark and rippling trunk, stripped down by time to a lascivious smoothness too stimulating to be legal."*

Arbutus likes rocky, well-drained soil, mild weather, and long droughts—a perfect match for the exposed bedrock, rain-shadowed Gulf and San Juan Islands. The tree is worthless as a resource, which has probably saved it—the grain is rock hard and twists, it warps and cracks and splits, seasons poorly, and it is subject to fungal infections (a delicate tree, really, it hates to have its roots disturbed, the soil around its trunk tamped in any way, or the slightest change in light). The largest arbutus in the archipelago is reputed to be on the north side of Thetis Island. Local artists and photographers have made Arbutus menziesii *a subject of many works of art—some quite erotic; look for them in galleries and at farmer's markets throughout the islands.*

GALIANO ISLAND

Galiano Islanders are a feisty, articulate lot. If an environmental protest is going on anywhere in North America, odds are better than even that a contingent from Galiano Island is involved. Though they number fewer than 1,000, Galiano Islanders have a long history of taking on developers and land speculators in the interests of preserving their little corner of paradise. In the process, they have built a strong, tight-knit community, where local politics and environmental issues dominate the most casual of gatherings. However, when we were there, the well-traveled places on the island seemed trampled and tired—perhaps because Galiano Island is first in line from the Vancouver metropolitan area. We suggest a visit off-season.

The island itself is long and narrow with no real village, just one cluster of shops and services (including the island's only fuel pumps) around Sturdies Bay, where the ferry lands, and another at the Georgeson Bay junction. There's no bank, no ATM, no laundromat.

In addition, there's no public water source on Galiano, and during the summer months, water is in short supply. Day visitors might consider bringing their own drinking water. If you're staying overnight, please be considerate of your host's limited supply.

"Galiano Islanders have won every environmental battle they've ever fought except for one. [Lumber giant] MacMillan Bloedel won development rights to build one house on every 20 acres they own."
—Tom Hennessey, island resident and naturalist

"We're surrounded by nature here— water, land, forest, and animal life. But what makes Galiano so wonderful is the people. They just care so much about the island, and what makes up the island way of life."
—Nancy Davidson, North Galiano Community Association

GETTING THERE

Galiano's only ferry terminal is at Sturdies Bay, on the northeast side of the island. Only 50 minutes from Tsawwassen by ferry, Galiano benefits from the most humane schedule among the islands. The mainland run that leaves Salt Spring at 6:30am, for example, picks up Galianans at a more reasonable 8:30am, depositing them in Tsawwassen an hour later. There are also numerous ferries from Vancouver Island's Swartz Bay—a trip that takes either one or two hours, depending on the number of scheduled stops.

Galiano is a popular weekend destination for Vancouverites due to its proximity to the city. Ferry reservations are highly recommended, and essential for Friday evenings. From Sturdies Bay, access to the other Outer Islands is quite good, which makes it a natural base of operations for island hopping.

Galiano has no garbage dump, so thoughtful visitors take their recyclables and so forth with them when they leave.

Throughout the year, islanders host a number of special events—dinners, dances, concerts, and performances, as likely to feature touring artists as local talent. Visitors are welcome to join these festivities, which usually benefit a worthy community effort. Look for notices on the many bulletin boards around the shops and the community hall on Sturdies Bay Road, or ask your innkeeper.

ACTIVITIES

Picnics. For basic food provisions, try the Corner Store and Galiano Liquor Agency, 250/539-2986, at Georgeson Bay and Sturdies Bay Roads. For a more eclectic grocery expedition, Daystar Market, 250/539-2505, across the street carries fresh produce and locally made, frequently organic, specialty items, including Haggis Farms breads (the best breads anywhere) and cookies from Saturna Island. They also have Starbucks coffee (a rare find in the Gulf Islands) and a good assortment of health foods, vitamins, and supplements.

Close to Sturdies Bay, on the south side of the island, is Bellhouse Park, a gentle, mossy expanse of land overlooking Active Pass to Mayne Island. This is the place to head with your newly packed lunch.

Arts and Crafts. Galiano is refreshingly free of crass commercialism. Dandelion Gallery of Fine Art (3-23 Madrona Drive, 250/539-5622), just around the corner from the ferry, is a good source for local arts and crafts. Schoenfeld Knives (139 Warbler Street, 250/539-2806) carries an impressive selection of handmade knives for camping, hunting, fishing, and the kitchen. Ixchel Craft Shop (at Georgeson Bay and Sturdies Bay Roads, and at Montague Harbour Marina, 250/539-3038) has a varied and imaginative stock of crafts from around the islands and around the world. Look for hand-painted clothing, musical instruments, jewelry, and Schoenfeld knives. Farmers and Artisans Market is every Friday during summer months at the South Galiano Community Hall, 250/539-2375.

GETTING AROUND

Go Galiano Island Shuttle provides van/taxi service from one end of Galiano Island to the other, 250/539-0202. They also rent buzzy little red scooters. You can rent bikes at Galiano Bicycle, 36 Burrill Road, near the ferry landing; 250/539-9906.

Catamaran Cruising. Tom and Ann Hennessey and daughter Kate, who operate Canadian Gulf Island Catamaran Cruises, 250/539-2930, must have discovered the secret to a 36-hour day. In addition to operating a busy bed-and-breakfast and an accommodations booking service, this peripatetic family also charters boating expeditions among the Gulf Islands. The mother ship is a 46-foot catamaran that can hold up to 25 passengers, 12 kayaks, and an undisclosed number of bicycles. Between April and October, the Hennesseys will tailor a boating expedition to your needs. A favorite trip is a four-hour nature sail to a bird sanctuary and secluded sandy beach accessible only by boat. Or try a combo sailing and kayaking trip, possibly with a bicycling component thrown in, from two to five days.

Camping. Montague Harbour is a lovely, sheltered bay with spectacular views over Trincomali Channel. For thousands of years before Europeans set foot on these islands, it was home to a thriving community of Coast Salish natives, who, at their height, outnumbered Galiano's current population. Look for the council trees—huge, ancient maples with generous, spreading boughs—where tribal elders would sit to hold court and dispense justice. This is a popular campground, with 40 campsites. During the summer and on holiday weekends, it's likely to be full. No hookups for RVs or trailers.

Marina. The only marina on Galiano is at Montague Harbour, 250/539-5733. The marina and store make a nice destination, though it's a bit of a hike from the ferry landing; you can cab or bicycle over. A picturesque clapboard-sided building stretches along the harbor's waterfront with the marina out front. Inside there's a well-stocked bookstore, Canterbury coffee and espresso, breakfast and lunch counter, ice cream, and a pleasant spot to eat on the deck overlooking the harbor.

Along Bodega Ridge and Dionisio Point Provincial Park, look for pelagic cormorants, double-crested cormorants, harlequin ducks, oystercatchers, peregrine falcons, pileated and hairy woodpeckers, and bald eagles, as well as many other species of sea and land birds.

There are well-marked trails up Mount Galiano and up Mount Sutil; however, the Sutil trailhead is accessible only by boat. Either route opens up superb vistas to the southwest of Vancouver Island, with views of the Olympic Mountains, 60 miles to the south.

There are also four government docks on the island, at Retreat Cove, Montague Harbour, Sturdies Bay, and Whaler Bay.

Kayaking. Ben Miltner began renting canoes on Galiano in 1983, and started Gulf Island Kayaking (also known as Galiano Island Kayaking) in 1985, one of the first kayak businesses in the islands. He's at Montague Harbour Marina, where he rents kayaks (his fleet of fiberglass sea kayaks is a good way to try out various makes and models) and canoes, and arranges day, multiday, and expedition-level guided tours; 250/539-2442. Lessons, too. All levels of experience welcome.

Tom and Ann Hennessey, who operate Southwind Sailing Charters, will also rent kayaks (Galiano Bay Sea Kayaking, 250/539-2930) by the hour or the week from Situl Lodge overlooking Montague Harbour. Two- to four-hour guided tours to surrounding islands and points of interest are offered. All levels of experience welcome; lessons.

Primitive Park. Dionisio Point Provincial Park, at the entrance to Polier Pass, has great views over Georgia Strait; it is one of the newest, and least tampered with, provincial parks in the Gulf Islands. To get there, follow Porlier Pass Road out to Cook Road, then turn off. Warning: The road into the park is primitive, but it's well worth the wear and tear on your car. There are a few camping spots, but little in the way of facilities. Bring prepared food and water—it's a long trek back to the grocery store. Absolutely no fires permitted.

Hiking. Bodega Ridge just may be the short answer to why Galiano Islanders are so tenacious about protecting their environment. The rocky bluff that runs along the spine of the island is unique in western Canada for its abundance and variety of wildflowers, forest vegetation, and wildlife and its spectacular coastal scenery. From the top of the ridge, you overlook broad vistas of islands all the way to the Olympic Mountains on one side and cathedral-like groves of old-growth Douglas fir on the other. There are several trails through the ridge, ranging from a short and easy half-hour walk to a more challenging four- or five-hour hike to Dionisio Point at the north end of the island. Access to the ridge is off Cottage Way, which is off Porlier Pass Road. Drive up the road, which is twisty and narrow, but otherwise in relatively good shape, and park at the top. Follow the trails up to the top of the ridge.

Fires are banned everywhere on Galiano from April 15 to October 15.

Horseback Riding. Bodega Ridge Rides at Bodega Resort, 250/539-2677, guides horseback tours through about 20 miles of some of the prettiest scenery in the islands. The horse trails are in a different part of Bodega Ridge from the walking trails. Rates are $15 an hour for a minimum group of two. Advance reservations aren't usually necessary, except in the case of larger parties (to a maximum of 9).

"You can go for a walk, or you can hang out at the pub."

—A local bartender

Biking. It has been estimated that 30 kilometers of island bicycling is the equivalent of 90 kilometers of bicycling on city streets. In short, this is a challenge best accepted by only the fittest. For rentals and repairs there's Galiano Bicycle (36 Burrill Road, 250/539-0202). They rent 21-speed mountain bikes for $29.95 a day. This is also the best source of information on off-road trails and low-traffic routes.

RESTAURANTS

LA BERENGERIE ☆

Popular with locals and visitors alike, this quaint 40-seat restaurant occupies the main floor of a two-story, wood-sided house, set back from the road amid huge cedars. Owner/chef/hotelier Huguette Benger, who learned the trade running a small hotel in Paris, offers a four-course menu that might include local venison with raisin sauce, and crisp Galiano-grown vegetables. The service and atmosphere are casual (Berger is often your server as well as your chef). Reservations are a must. In July and August, there's a vegetarian-only outdoor dining cafe on the deck out back for lazy afternoons (see Cafe Boheme, below). There are four modest guest rooms, two with private baths and all with paper-thin walls. The hot tub on the deck up at Benger's house and the good breakfast make up for any flaws. *Montague Harbour Rd (corner of Clanton Rd), Galiano Island, BC V0N 1P0; 250/539-5392; $$; full bar; V; checks OK; lunch, dinner every day (Thurs–Sun, off-season; closed Nov–Mar).*

CAFE BOHEME

New on Galiano, Cafe Boheme is an offshoot of the island's well-loved La Berengerie. Really nothing more elaborate than a few tables set in the garden when the weather permits (so far it's open only during July and August), this little outdoor bistro offers great, strictly vegetarian food, the best people-watching vantage point on the island, and prices that bring back change from a $10 bill. *Montague Harbour Rd (corner of Clanton Road), Galiano Island, BC V0N 1P0; 250/539-5392; $; beer and wine; no credit cards; local checks only; lunch, dinner every day, seasonally.*

HUMMINGBIRD INN

Along with hearty pub food, draft beer, and reasonable prices, you get billiard tables, darts, and occasional live music in a rustic garden setting (one of the prettiest in the islands) and comfortable seating outside in the summer. The atmosphere is sociable year-round, but particularly so in the summer months, when backpackers and campers swell Galiano's population. *47 Sturdies Bay Rd, Galiano Island, BC V0N 1P0; 250/539-5472; $; beer and wine; AE, MC, V; no checks; open every day.*

LODGINGS

THE BELLHOUSE INN ☆ ☆

This turn-of-the-century farmhouse, run as an inn from the 1920s to the 1960s, has been renovated by Andrea Porter and David Birchall and is once again an inn. Its 6 acres look out on Active Pass; you can watch the ferries and the whales from one of Galiano's rare sand beaches, lie in a hammock under the plum tree, or feed apples to the small flock of sheep—their wool is used for the duvets at Bellhouse. Just around the corner is Bellhouse Park, an ideal location for a slow walk. The Kingfisher is the best of the rooms, with a fine view out over the pass and a Jacuzzi for overcycled muscles. Also on the property is a duplex cabin; each side has two bedrooms, a kitchen, a sitting area, and a patio with a view. Breakfast specialty of the house is Eggs Bellhouse, eggs

Benedict with salmon and shrimp standing in for ham. Arrive in style: David can pick you up from the ferry in a 1935 Bentley. You can continue the mood by playing croquet on the lawn, sipping a glass of sherry, and sampling Andrea's tart and very English lemon curd. *29 Farmhouse Rd (from ferry terminal, up the hill, left on Burrill, left on Jack), PO Box 16, Site 4, Galiano Island, BC V0N 1P0; 800/970-7464 or 250/539-5667; bellhouse@gulfislands.com; www.monday.com/bellhouse; $$$; MC, V; checks OK.*

BODEGA RESORT ☆

On a high, westward-facing bluff in the center of Galiano is a western-style resort, ideal for families or large, casual groups. There are seven two-story log chalets, with fir and cedar paneling and touches such as lace country curtains, custom cherrywood cabinets, and cast-iron stoves. Each has three bedrooms, 1½ baths, a fully equipped kitchen, and two view decks; the ranch-style unit has one bath and a large sun deck surrounded by a rose garden. The lodge has a conference room and a few additional rooms. For fun, there's horseback riding, a trout pond, hiking trails, and Bodega Ridge and Dionisio Point nearby. Turn your back on the recently logged hillside and soak up the unobstructed views to the west. *20 Monasty Rd (follow Porlier Pass Rd 22½ km/14 miles north of Sturdies Bay to Cook Rd, then to Monasty Rd), PO Box 115, Galiano Island, BC V0N 1P0; 250/539-2677; $$; MC, V; checks OK.*

CLIFF PAGODA BED AND BREAKFAST ☆

The Asian-style Cliff Pagoda, which looks as if it were plucked from Beijing's Forbidden City, is described by its builders, Rick and Brigette Finnie, as a sort of Japanese country inn with a West Coast flair—lots of glass, open space, and built-in cushioned seating. The Cliff Pagoda stands out for its design, amenities, and breathtaking view of Montague Harbour and Park Island. Bicyclists may struggle up the long dirt driveway ¼ mile, but they're rewarded with a spectacular view. Six rooms are small and bathrooms are shared (except for one room that has its own private bath), but there's a large porch and communal hot tub—so why stay in your room? *2851 Montague Harbour Rd, Galiano*

"This is probably one of the last places in North America where people just talk to each other, without any particular motive, and without looking at their watches."
—Ann Hennessey, B&B proprietor

Island, BC V0N 1P0; 250/539-2260; www.wowsites.com/cliff_pagoda; $; MC, V; no checks.

MOONSHADOWS ★★

It's a modern house, with a spacious, sparsely furnished living room large enough for classical music concerts in front of the stone fireplace. Hardwood floors and French doors warm the house. Living room and deck overlook 2 private acres and a broad meadow—and there's always a sack of cracked corn for this spring's ducklings, the waddling hens, and one cranky drake, "Rambo." Upstairs guest rooms are large and at opposite ends of the house, each with its own bathroom. The best guest room is on the first floor: a very private garden suite with huge tiled shower and deep whirlpool tub, with room for two, overlooking the garden—altogether almost 500 square feet to yourself. French doors lead to a private deck covered with glass. For breakfast, Pat Goodwin bakes frittatas, casseroles, Dutch and French pancakes, and soufflés, served with platters heaped with fruit plus lots of hot coffee. An extra service: owner Dave Muir owns the island's only shuttle service, Go Galiano, and you can talk him into taking you and your whole family (he has a van for larger groups) just about anywhere. *771 Georgeson Bay Rd (S16, C16, RR1), Galiano, BC V0N 1P0; 888/666-6742 or 250/539-5544; moonshadowsbb@bc.sympatico.ca; $$; MC, V; no checks.*

MOUNT GALIANO EAGLE'S NEST ★★

 Just about the time you think you must have turned onto a logging road by mistake, you finally come upon Francine Renaud and Bernard Mignault's unusual home, nestled in its roost at the foot of Mount Galiano with an eagle's-eye view of Trincomali Channel. Built from a combination of slash wood and salvaged architectural elements, the house sits on 75 acres of land and a whole kilometer of waterfront—all abutting the Galiano Mountain Wilderness Park. Renaud and Mignault's garden is a work of art (and a prolific producer). And the breakfasts: melon and grapefruit served with nasturtium blossoms, followed by waffles accompanied by all manner of toppings. Our favorite of the three rooms is the romantic, peach-colored upstairs chamber, now with an adjoining room that makes a suite suitable for a family. A new room with glassed-in front looks out over the gardens and the water; the third room has a loft. This place is an absolute treat unless you have something against shared bathrooms or friendly cats. *2-720 Active Pass Dr (call for directions), Galiano Island, BC V0N 1P0; 250/539-2567; www.victoriabc.com/accom/mgaliano.htm; $$$; V; checks OK.*

WOODSTONE COUNTRY INN

Host and co-owner Andrew Nielsen-Pich is anxious to indulge guests, and the reasonable prices make this inn one of the best values in upper-end accommodation on the Gulf Islands. It's not on the water, but the setting, overlooking a field and forest, is still perfectly relaxing. Business retreats are encouraged (one of the rooms can be converted to a small conference room); children are not. The 12 rooms, all redone in bold rose and pink chintz, are spacious and bright, with tall windows, sitting areas, private baths (some with Jacuzzis or soaker tubs), and such touches as hand-stenciled wallpaper or original artwork. All have fireplaces. In the comfortable common room are a piano and well-stocked bookshelves. For breakfast (included in the rate), expect something rich and delicious; in the afternoon, guests regroup for tea.

The dining room here ranks high: chef and co-owner Gail Nielsen-Pich tempts with a reasonably priced table d'hôte dinner, which can include such specialties as a savory cheese and tomato strudel, breast of duck with red wine and rhubarb sauce, swordfish with caperberry butter, or vegetarian dishes such as artichoke and mushroom pie with Italian caponata. Desserts are outstanding; Galiano residents would stage a full-scale rebellion if the bread pudding with rum sauce disappeared from the menu. *Georgeson Bay Rd (bear left off Sturdies Bay Rd, follow signs to turnoff); RR 1, Galiano Island, BC V0N 1P0; 250/539-2022; $$$; full bar; AE, MC, V; no checks; dinner every day (closed Jan).*

SATURNA ISLAND

Remote, sparsely populated, and difficult to get to, Saturna Island is easily the most beautiful and unspoiled of the Gulf Islands. This is the ultimate get-away-from-it-all experience. You'll find no little craft boutiques, no souvenir stands, only two options for dining out, and precious few other amenities here. Saturna harbors pristine wilderness and a picturesque village, Boot Cove, the island's center of population. Islanders have mixed feelings about tourism. On the one hand, bed-and-breakfast proprietors have a vested interest in maintaining the flow. On the other, locals are understandably reluctant to compromise the elements that make Saturna such a magical place. Gulf Islanders generally cherish their privacy, and this seems to be more true on Saturna than elsewhere. While there has been some discussion about setting aside a portion of Winter Cove Marine Provincial Park for camping, islanders have been adamant in their objections. Note that there is no overnight camping anywhere on the island. Similarly, there aren't any rental facilities for bicycles or kayaks. Bring your own, or settle in with a good book (and if you plan to spend the night, be sure to make advance reservations).

Located east of Saturna Island, off the northeast coast of Tumbo Island, Cabbage Island offers anchorage on its south side that is appropriate for short stays or overnights, although it is exposed to easterly and westerly winds. The sandy beach is one for sunbathing and swimming. There are picnic, camping, and toilet facilities.

ACTIVITIES

Shopping. Opportunities for spending money on Saturna are severely limited, which may make this the most economical vacation spot in North America. Gallery Rosa has paintings, prints, and local pottery; glass and other arts and crafts from the Outer Gulf Islands; as well as Jacques Campbell's washable sheepskins from his Saturna Island farm. The gallery is a five-minute walk from the ferry. Open weekends, noon to 4pm or by appointment, 250/539-2866.

Picnics. Aside from the two basic grocery stores, you can pick up bread and wine from the baker and the vintner. Islanders rave about Haggis Farm Bakery (Narvaez Bay Road, 250/539-2591), which offers the best and freshest organic breads and cookies available anywhere. Look for the first driveway past the cemetery, but note that bakers work at night and early morning, and may not be there when you are. Saturna Island Vineyards, on the island's south end, overlooks the San Juan Islands

The roads are steep and most are unpaved, so bring your bike. While Saturna is the most rugged of the Gulf Islands, the payoff is that bikers rarely buck traffic, even in summer. When exploring Saturna by bike, please stick to the roads. The island has a small section of crown (public) land, but access to it is through private property.

GETTING THERE

Lyall Harbour is the ferry terminal for Saturna. A very complicated schedule of ferries services Saturna from Mayne, Galiano, and Pender; but basically access is via either Village Bay on Mayne Island, which is the transfer point for Saturna from the other islands, or Swartz Bay. For a small fee, you may be able to hitch an early morning or late afternoon ride with the water taxi from Salt Spring as it picks up and delivers high school students (all Outer Island public school students commute by water taxi to Salt Spring). This is an option only during the school year on school days, and only if space permits. For schedules and to verify space availability, phone Gulf Island Water Taxi, 250/537-2510

Viable Marine Services (Box 45, Saturna, BC V0N 2Y0, 250/539-3200) offers water taxi services to Vancouver Island's Swartz Bay, and they'll pick up passengers from (and return them to) any of the southern Gulf Islands. They can also transport bicycles or kayaks. Dress warmly. .

Don your scuba gear and look for giant sea anemones off Elliot Bluff, at the southeast end of Saturna. Java Islets, near here, offer kelp beds, abalone, and sea urchins, and one of the Gulf Islands' nicest dives.

and Mount Baker on a clear day. Wines, wine tasting, seminars, and wine paraphernalia are available here, along with picnic lunches to eat in the vineyard. Open June 1 through the first weekend in October. Call for hours; 250/539-5139.

Hiking. Mount Warburton Pike (a pike is a hill with a pointed summit) dominates the landscape on the south side of the island, its barren south slope clearly visible across Plumper Sound from points on the Penders, Salt Spring, and Vancouver Islands. Access is off Harris Road, which crosses Narvaez Bay Road, then a sharp left up Staples Road. For the next 4 kilometers (the road is rough, so you may prefer to walk) you'll pass through an ecological preserve of old-growth Douglas fir, wildflowers, ferns, and mushrooms roughly the size of dinner plates. At the peak, alas, the 20th century intrudes with a particularly ugly assemblage of radio and television receiving equipment. Never mind. Turn your back on this mess and walk toward the bluffs along the Brown Ridge Nature Trail. This may not be Everest, but there's a definite sensation of being at the top of the world, with a dazzling array of islands, ocean, and mainland laid out at your feet. Keep an eye open for feral crofter goats—rare remnants of a breed brought to the island in the 19th century. They are shy, but they're known to graze on the mountainside.

Beach Walking. Winter Cove Marine Provincial Park includes more than 2 kilometers of shoreline that follows the eastern side of the cove around the point to the north side of the island, looking across the Strait of Georgia. East Point Beach, exactly 1 kilometer from the junction of Winter Cove Road and East Point Road, is a naturalist's paradise. Follow the narrow lane down to the tiny beach, which is strewn with lots of driftwood. Walk north from here for more good views over the strait.

From East Point Beach, follow East Point Road out to the point. If at all possible, time your trip to coincide with low tide. Park your car (or bike) outside the lighthouse gates and walk down the steep slope to a shell-and-gravel beach. Ah, sheer wildness. The sandstone rock faces could have been carved by Henry Moore on steroids. Tidal pools teem with marine life in a wild kaleidoscope of colors and shapes: sea anemones, spider crabs, hermit crabs, limpets, periwinkles, mussels, barnacles, sea stars, and a host of other creatures. The kelp beds that swirl around the tip of the point nurture a smorgasbord of delicacies for loons, grebes, cormorants, bald eagles, oystercatchers, terns, and more. Harbor seals, sea lions, and orcas feed on the salmon that gather in the eddies around the point.

From the ferry landing, follow Narvaez Bay Road to the end of Harris Road and walk the Quarry Trail to Thomson Park. You can also walk from Narvaez Bay Road to the head of Lyall Harbour's beach—a nice "warm" place for a swim.

Goings On. Saturna's big social event of the year is a lamb bake, which happens on Canada Day (July 1). Follow East Point to Winter Cove Marine Provincial Park, the site of Saturna's justifiably famous Canada Day Lamb Barbecue, and arguably the most beautiful spot on Saturna. Saturna Islanders put on the community fund-raiser every year, and between 1,200 and 2,000 people from all over the islands, the mainland, and even Washington State show up for the daylong party. For the event, islanders roast 28 lambs Argentinean style. (Don't ask— islanders won't say. You have to show up to find out what an Argentinean-style barbecue is.) There are games of all sorts,

Throughout the islands, shellfish might be contaminated by "red tide"—high concentrations of a toxic marine alga that can cause paralytic shellfish poisoning in the unwary user. For a red tide update, and to inquire about limits and other regulations, phone the Fisheries office in Duncan; 250/746-6221.

Aside from being a wonderful spot for beachcombing or sunbathing, Winter Cove Park is home to a variety of wildlife, including migrating ducks, black-tailed deer, raccoons, mink, and river otters. Harbor seals and sea lions come into the bay to feed, and, though there are no guarantees, you might see a pod of orcas frolicking in the distance.

East Point is one of the best spots for fishing in the Gulf Islands. It is a favorite spot for angling, drift fishing, and trolling. Spring salmon and coho pass Saturna Point, lingering in Lyall Harbour at select times of the year. You can troll, drift fish, or cast from the government wharf.

including nail-driving contests. Those who want to join in the free festivities (or indulge in the lamb feed, for a nominal fee) are encouraged to come. Get there by noon, and if possible get there by water. There is excellent moorage at Winter Cove, and islanders have organized a water-shuttle service between the park and the ferry. For those who are aquaphobic, land transportation service is also provided.

Other annual events, held at the island's community hall, are pig roasts in May and November, and Crabfest at Easter. Robbie Burns Night is a traditional sit-down ribald feast for 85 in gray January, celebrating the Scot poet's womanizing nature, with bagpipes, kilts, Scottish dance, and poetry. The center is also transformed to a performance hall for the semi-annual productions of Theatre on the Rock.

Boating. Lyall Harbour has a government wharf for short-term moorage as space permits (fishing boats always have priority at government wharves), fuel supplies, and a grocery store. Winter Cove is well protected and provides one of the best anchorages on the island, but it is relatively shallow and reefs partially block the western entrance; careful navigation is required. Small boats can enter from the Strait of Georgia through Boat Passage, a narrow channel with strong tides. In calm weather, you can anchor overnight at Boot Cove, though the surrounding land is private property, with little access to the shore. Breezy Bay has good anchorage, sheltered from southeast winds. At the eastern end of the island, there is temporary moorage at Bruce Bight, Narvaez Bay, and Fiddlers Cove, but the shorelines here are steep and forbidding.

The boat launch at Winter Cove is an ideal starting point for exploring the maze of islands between Saturna and Mayne.

RESTAURANTS

LIGHTHOUSE PUB

 For a casual nosh, head to the Lighthouse Pub, beside the ferry terminal and below the Saturna store, for lunch and hearty dinner specials. The food is so-so at best, but on Saturna, alternative dining opportunities are severely limited. While the atmosphere is a trifle rough around the edges, the setting—with its views of Lyle Harbour, home to an abundance of seals—is out-and-out gorgeous. *102 East Point Rd,*

Saturna Island, BC V0N 2Y0; 250/539-5725; $; MC, V; no checks; open every day.

SATURNA LODGE ★★

 This resort (formerly Boot Cove) has changed names, owners, managers, and chefs in the last few years and has finally regained a reputation for reliability and good food. The elegant but casual country inn is now owned by Larry and Robyn Page, who also own Saturna Vineyard. The lovely frame lodge sits high on a hill overlooking an inlet and an oyster farm. Windows wrap around the simple, comforting dining room; a crackling fire makes it even more inviting on a cool evening. Chef Hubertus Surm, of Vancouver, entices diners to boat in from other islands to take advantage of the prix-fixe menu—one of the best deals on the islands, at $25 for three courses, three choices with each course—and the limited but well-chosen wine list. On a given evening, you might choose from prawns, salad, or soup; halibut in mustard sauce, chicken breast stuffed with spinach, or three-cheese pasta; hazelnut chocolate cake, crêpes Chantilly, or fresh herbed goat cheese. The seven bright and sunny B&B rooms upstairs are contemporary in feel, with pleasant sitting areas and serene views. All have private baths; the honeymoon suite ($160) has a soaker tub and private balcony. Reservations for meals and accommodations are essential. There's guest pickup from (and delivery to) the Saturna ferry dock. *130 Payne Rd (follow signs from ferry), PO Box 54, Saturna Island, BC V0N 2Y0; 888/539-8800 or 250/539-2254; www.saturna-island.bc.ca; $$–$$$; full bar; MC, V; no checks; lunch, dinner every day in summer; dinner Thurs–Sun in winter.*

Saturna Islanders take their privacy seriously, but the quiet, scenic roads offer spectacular opportunities for walks.

THETIS ISLAND

"You can't be addicted to nightlife if you're going to live on an island."
—Janet Comstock, B&B proprietor.

Access to Thetis Island is from Chemainus, 90 minutes north of Victoria on Vancouver Island, a charming little waterfront town that made itself over from a rough logging/mill town to one of Vancouver's most popular tourist towns by cleaning up and painting the town with 32 murals. Thetis Island, 45 minutes away by ferry, is all privately owned. Bring your bike and pedal the whole 20 miles of road on the island; you'll probably have them to yourself. Thetis is adjacent to Kuper Island, which is entirely Native reserve land. The ferry stops at both islands, but you've got to have formal permission from the Natives to get off the boat on Kuper.

ACTIVITIES

Good Eats. Real old-fashioned cake doughnuts, fried in oil. You can pick them up by dinghy at Blue Heron Donuts, 250/246-9602, at the end of Blue Heron Road, Tuesday to Saturday; or walk there from the ferry (it's a hike). You can rent a Necky kayak from Troy Kasting at Overbury Farm Resort (the farm has been in the family for four generations) 250/246-9769, and paddle round the island. However you get there, you'll have earned your delicious little sugary (yum) dough ball.

If warm doughnuts aren't enough incentive to visit Thetis Island, try this: walk on the ferry and hike from the landing to Telegraph Harbour Marina (look for signs) for a hand-dipped old-fashioned milk shake. From there, take off across the island for about a mile to Clam Bay Cottage, 250/246-1016, for afternoon tea. If "tea" brings to mind high tea in the Empress Hotel, forget about it; this is Island Tea, served by Donna Kaiser in the informal garden of her very pretty little B&B on the waterfront. Donna is down-to-earth, has raised a houseful of kids, and is a professional caterer specializing in weddings in her own garden. Her afternoon tea consists of petite sandwiches, salmon and leek quiche tartlet, scones with clotted cream and strawberry jam, candied ginger cookies, lemon pound cake, and a pot of tea, for $12.95 per person. Or you can drop by from 7 to 9pm each night for "Just Desserts:" cheesecake covered with fresh blueberries, old-fashioned chocolate cake, lemon mousse with blackberry *coulis*, orange sherbet meringue (a Baked Alaska for one), or whatever else Donna dreams up. Her B&B is in a modern house with a cottage next door—all facing south. When we were there guests sprawled in Adirondack-style chairs along the waterfront, limply relaxing.

"Living on an island really forces you to develop your imagination."
—Frances Faminow, artist

Arts and Crafts. The Spinning Wheel Fibre Works and Studio, as well as Thetis Island Alpaca Ranch, offer the work of local knitters. You can get a guided tour of the ranch, studio, and carding/spinning process Wednesdays or Saturdays during the summer for $4 per person, or look around for free. Nice Jepson, 250/246-2555, specializes in raku pottery; Veronica Shelford's pottery studio, 250/246-1509, overlooking the water, is open by appointment, as is Simone Weber-Luckham's sculpture studio, 250/246-4802.

Farm and Garden. Thetis Island Salads (402 Kenwood, 250/246-4042) delivers bags of rare heirloom lettuces and greens, herbs, and flowers to your boat (or the ferry landing) for $5 a bag, noon to dusk.

GABRIOLA ISLAND

While not usually considered one of the Gulf Islands (though we certainly don't know why it isn't), Gabriola merits at least a few hours in your itinerary, if only to explore the Malaspina Galleries (an eerie natural rock formation) or to search for hidden petroglyphs, of which there are thousands. Just 20 minutes by ferry from Nanaimo on Vancouver Island, Gabriola Island seems to be in real danger of becoming another casualty of urban sprawl. There's more evidence of raw, new growth and development here than on any of the other islands, which makes for a better level of services, but could as easily destroy anything of value or charm.

During the day, ferries from Nanaimo to Descanso Bay on Gabriola depart every hour on the half hour. In the late afternoon through evening, they depart at quarter to the hour. Ferries return to Nanaimo on the hour, and at quarter after the hour in the afternoon. Round-trip fare is $11.25; 250/669-1211.

ACTIVITIES

Shopping. The main shopping area for Gabriola is the Folklife Village (at Lochinvar Lane and North Road, across from the RCMP station). The center is more interesting for its architecture than for its shopping opportunities. Visitors to Expo '86 in Vancouver may remember the massive cedar post-and-beam structure as the venue for that fair's folklife exhibits. Transposed to Gabriola, it is a handsome addition to the island, though it now houses a predictable assortment of services (including the island's only bank machine). FOGO Folk Art is filled with whimsical furniture (such as stools with chaps or feet with bunions) and life-size carved wooden folk in a variety of silly postures and outfits, 250/247-8082. Raspberry's Books and Beverages, 250/247-9959, is a good bookstore/cappuccino bar. In addition, there's an excellent craft gallery (Village Craftworks, 250/247-7412) and two better-than-average women's clothing stores (the Wooden Hanger Clothing Company, 250/247-8599, and Soda Creek Clothing Company, 250/247-8812). For an eclectic choice of books, maps, charts, and items related to boats and boating, check out Page's Marina on Silva Bay (at the end of Coast Road, 250/247-8931).

"Gabriola gives us a lifestyle well within our means, and it's a safe and healthy environment for children. We can control what influences them here."
—Margo Kemble, resident

"What I like about Gabriola is basically the people. Everybody helps everybody else here."
—Sue deCarteret, editor, the Gabriola Sounder

Gabriola's museum, 250/247-9987, located at the top of the hill above the ferry landing, provides an overview of the island's natural history, pioneer past, and native arts and culture. Open only on weekend afternoons.

Goings On. On the last Saturday in April, Gabriola hosts the Outhouse Race, a hilarious and elaborate competition among the island's volunteer fire department, service clubs, and retailers, held to benefit various charities. The race usually finishes with a gala dance at the community hall. The third Saturday in August is set aside for the Salmon Barbecue, a popular fundraiser for the community hall. The party takes place at the hall on South Road, toward Degnen Bay, and includes games, musicians, and, of course, a feast of barbecued salmon. In September, Gabriolans celebrate the end of summer with Gabriola Days, a weekend of revelry that includes softball tournaments, games, a street dance, and other special events geared toward the islanders rather than tourists.

Throughout the winter months, Page's Marina (on Silva Bay, 250/247-8931) plays host to an informal and irregularly scheduled series of poetry readings, concerts, and discussion groups.

Beach Walking. Gabriola has an impressive variety of beaches. Clamber down to the one at Sandwell Park. Dedicated access is off Pirate's Hollow, Zola Road, and Zelta Road. If your fitness level resembles that of a tuberous vegetable, you may want the easier access at Berry Point. Follow Schooner Road, Barnacle Road, Windham Road, or Tarbert Road. Not officially designated as a public beach, the shoreline at the end of Whalebone Drive is one of the last few natural wilderness beaches left in the islands. Drumbeg Park at the south end also boasts a fine beach that is easily accessible once you've found the park. Follow South Road to Coast Road, turn right, then right again at Stalker Road, drive for ¾ kilometer, and turn left onto the one-lane access road.

Just up the road from the ferry is the old Millstone Quarry, which has fascinating freshwater pools filled with a variety of little critters.

For clam beds, tidal pools, and a picnic among the old brickworks, there's Brickyard Beach at the foot of Ferne Road, on False Narrows.

LOCAL NEWS

Gabriola Island boasts not one, not two, but three newspapers. Reading the local press is an instant, if cursory, education in the social dynamics of a community. This is where you'll find details on local events, points of interest, and bones of contention. The Gabriola Sounder, published biweekly, is the island's newspaper of record—a respectable, responsible gray broadsheet. And then there's the Flying Shingle, published monthly, which is unapologetically opinionated—almost to the point of being libelous and gossipy. It has been an island must-read for 28 years and counting. Check out Wavelengths, a kayak magazine published on Gabriola and distributed free all over Canada and the western coast of the United States.

Trails branch to the right and the left. The swimming here is reputedly good, but the currents through Gabriola Pass are swift and treacherous. Page's Marina (at the end of Coast Road on Silva Bay, 250/247-8931) publishes a helpful, clearly written guide to walks on the island. It sells for $1—a worthwhile investment.

Petroglyphs. Gabriola Island is an important archaeological site, and thousands of petroglyphs can be found all over the island. Non-natives don't know who carved these rocks, when, or why; if the Natives know, they're keeping this to themselves. Some petroglyphs are uncovered and in plain view; many more are still hidden under layers of moss. We suggest you not go digging around them. To view the most accessible of these rock carvings, follow South Road for about 10 kilometers from the ferry to the United Church, then pick up the trail behind the church. Do not take rubbings or disturb the petroglyphs in any way.

Camping. There are only two places to camp on the island. Page's Marina (at the end of Coast Road on Silva Bay, 250/247-8931) has ten sites, four with electricity, that are best for tents and small vans, as well as five cottages. Closer to the ferry terminal, the Gabriola Campground has 28 sites on Taylor Bay Road, 250/247-2079.

Malaspina Galleries. Turn left onto Taylor Bay Road from the ferry terminal, and follow this road down to Malaspina Drive to the Malaspina Galleries, a spectacular sandstone formation carved by time, wind, and sea action. Turn right, and take Malaspina down to the parking lot. From here, there's a short trail out to the point and the Galleries, which resemble giant waves cresting over the shoreline. You can explore the cave-like sculptures freely, but be careful—the rocks can be very slippery, particularly when wet.

Kayaking. Gabriola Cycle and Kayaks, 250/247-8277, rents kayaks but not bicycles—that part of their name refers to 10-day off-island tours in wintertime hot spots they organize. They also organize some weekend kayak tours around Gabriola, Valdes Island, and Pirate's Cove; plus they lead more ambitious kayak tours in Johnson Strait, around the Queen

Relative to the other islands, Gabriola's topography is gentle. A good network of off-road trails criss-crosses the island. The island has no bike rental or repair shops, so bring your own bike and patch kit.

HighTest Dive Charters, 250/247-9753, arranges diving and wildlife observation charters for groups of six or more. You can make arrangements through your local dive shop. Gabriola Reefs Dive Shop at Silva Bay, 250/247-8443, rents equipment, supplies air, and guides diving expeditions.

Gabriola Golf and
Country Club (on
South Road,
250/247-8822) has
a lovely and chal-
lenging nine-hole,
par-71 course near
the island's only
large freshwater
lake.

Charlotte Islands, and off the west coast of Vancouver Island. Kayak rentals and limited instruction are available.

There are government docks at Degnen Bay and on False Narrows. Commercial marinas are Page's Marina, 250/247-8931, and the Boatel, 250/247-9351, both on Silva Bay.

RESTAURANTS

There's a dearth of interesting restaurant options on Gabriola, but probably no more so than on other islands. Islanders generally head to Nanaimo for a night out. Allegro Café, 250/247-2077, in Folklife Village, gets local raves for a great selection of breakfast and lunch items and fine dining at night with chef Tim Cosbey, formerly of Bishops in Vancouver. White Hart Pub, at the ferry landing, 250/247-8588, is a good choice for burgers and brews; a deck overlooks the water. Windecker's Restaurant (560 North Road, 250/247-2010), in a charming country-style house, offers family-style cooking. The resort and conference center Haven by the Sea (near the Malaspina Galleries, 250/247-9211) has a buffet-style dinner by reservation only. The Surf Lodge, 250/247-9231, has terrific views and good pub fare. At the island's south end, The Latitudes, 250/247-8662, is open only in the summers, but serves up gourmet fare for the yachting crowd. The adjoining Bitter End Pub, 250/247-8606, offers very good pub fare and is open year-round.

LODGINGS

SURF LODGE

 This rustic wood and stone lodge is across from the beach on the northwest shore of Gabriola Island. You'll find a very relaxed, comfortable atmosphere, a great stone fireplace in the lodge's sitting room, a saltwater pool, and outdoor recreational facilities. Accommodations include rooms and cabins, some with kitchens. The lodge has a restaurant and pub. *855 Berry Point Rd (at the island's north end), RR 1, Site 1, C17, Gabriola Island, BC V0R 1X0; 250/247-9231; www.gabriolaisland.org/surflodge; $; MC, V; no checks.*

Silver Blue
Charters, 250/247-
8807, offers year-
round salmon
fishing from a 22-
foot boat for up to
four passengers.
Tackle and licenses
are available
onboard. Also
available is a 28-
foot boat for up to
eight people for
fishing or sight-
seeing.

INDEX

BEST PLACES®
DESTINATIONS
SAN JUAN & GULF ISLANDS
REPORT FORM

Based on my personal experience, I wish to nominate the following restaurant or place of lodging; or confirm/correct/disagree with the current review.

_____

_____

_____

_____

(Please include address and telephone number of establishment, if convenient.)

REPORT

Please describe food, service, style, comfort, value, date of visit, and other aspects of your experience; continue on another piece of paper if necessary.

_____

_____

_____

_____

_____

_____

_____

I am not concerned, directly or indirectly, with the management or ownership of this establishment.

_____
SIGNED

_____
ADDRESS

_____

_____
PHONE   DATE

Please address to Best Places Destinations and send to:

SASQUATCH BOOKS
615 Second Avenue, Suite 260
Seattle, WA 98104
Feel free to email feedback as well: books@sasquatchbooks.com